Waking up from the American Dream

Book III:
KEEPING IT REAL

MICHELE MAINGOT CABRAL

Other books in the series:

Waking up from the American Dream
Book I: Walking Away
Book II: Making it Home

Customer Reviews on Amazon.com:

"Reader beware, be bold as you take this journey with Michele and Mike. Dare to go slowly, mindfully and introspectively as you trek long the path. You will explore freedom of choice, personal challenge, self-empowerment and self-sufficiency. You will consider the importance of connectedness, simplifying, balance, and place in life. As you get closer to the Cabral cabin in the woods you will embrace human capacity for hard work, creativity and spirituality."
-Rosemarie Laurent

"[*Walking* Away] reflects a genuine reverence for nature and a concomitant call to good stewardship. Featured characters include the author's constant companions, Hermes, her guiding light Orion's Sirius, hot pickled milkweed (naturally), random Mormons and ubiquitous black-flies."
-Giovanna

"Though I am a city girl, Cabral's book [*Making it Home*] brings me into a simple yet complex life…the joy of being in tune with the natural world. I long to experience this. Her book is so well-written and engages the reader with a full array of sensory experiences."
-Lisa Lefkow

ISBN-13: 1722846060
ISBN -10: 1722846062

To the blessings yet to come.

ACKNOWLEDGEMENTS

While writing a book may seem like a solitary process, it actually is not. I could never have written a single page if it weren't for the people who first encouraged me to write, my parents and family members (aunts and uncles – and let's face it, some months these people are the only reason I get a royalty check). Then there are the friends and neighbors who have agreed to appear in my books because they are just wonderful people.

Next up are the key friends who agree to give me feedback and point out errors: they are Consuelo Maingot, Kathy Doore, and Karla DeMaris. These folks are especially vital since most writers can ramble about things that aren't that important and they have to search out kind ways to say, "Hey, knock it off and get back to the story here!"

I would like to again thank my mother, Consuelo Maingot for taking the cover photo last summer when she visited with my father. If you did not notice, my mom is in every paragraph of these acknowledgements. I could never thank her enough, but I do try.

And of course, I have to thank my twin star, Mike, who has been the best friend a girl could ever ask for. And that is real.

CONTENTS

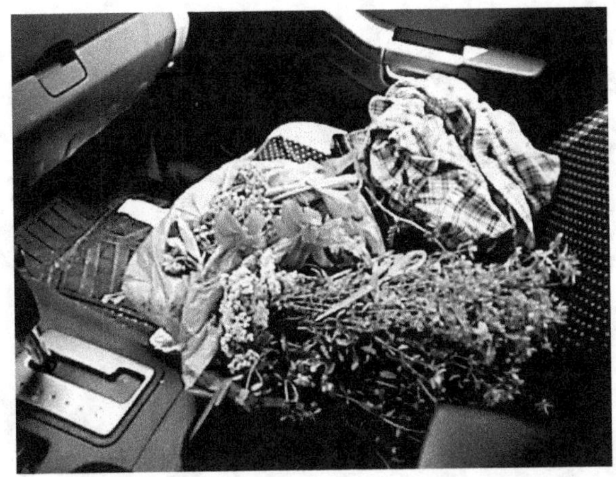

A FORAGER'S CODE OF ETHICS

1. Only take 1/3 of any plant or group of plants.
2. Always harvest from the outer branches or leaves as you would when pruning.
3. Don't eat all of a plant's seeds. If you harvest mushrooms, brush them off to leave spores.
4. Always ask permission from landowners.
5. When people tell you about a spot they forage, don't tell others.
6. Be respectful and thankful, offering something you value in return. (Native Americans use tobacco and cornmeal, but it could be the offering of a prayer, a few deep breaths, or the time to take it all in.)
7. Forage for what you can use or for what someone you know needs. Avoid an attitude of consumerism. It can lead to overharvesting.
8. Remember that all beings have their seasons. If a species is scarce, let it replenish itself.
9. All beings give. Remember to give.

Prologue
January 13, 2016

Yesterday I received a text message from my youngest daughter that made me smile. She had met a man through work who told her that he felt naïve for wanting to move out into nature and start his own garden.

"I told him not to fear," she messaged. "I shared with him your story and recommended your books to him.

"Thank you for being so real, Mimo."

"That's funny," I texted back, "I'm putting the finishing touches on book III and have decided to call it *Keeping it Real.*

Finishing up *Making it Home* was not as powerful a feeling as it was when we launched *Walking Away.* Some was the fact that it was an intensely personal book about adjusting to a new lifestyle that I had always dreamed about but had never considered would be difficult.

Exposing my inner thoughts and feelings were not new experiences. Sharing them in such a public and indelible way made me want to hide. When there were not many people at some of my book launchings for Book II, I tried not to internalize it.

Mike's comment was, "Well, it's more of a *chickie* kind of book. Don't worry about it." I could never get a read on whether he even liked Book II. But, it is a recording of what we went through, unplugged, so it stays.

That was his answer. I couldn't expect anything more from him. He's not the *chickie* kind of guy that would try and ameliorate my feelings, well ...not in the typical way. He did offer up some advice. "You got to just keep wigglin' your worm, little one, just keep wigglin' your worm."

That is just the type of encouragement I get from Mike. It makes sense to me. The whole act of fishing isn't so much about what you reel in. It's more about being out there and sometimes loving the way the fish playfully jump just beyond your reach.

Waking up from the American Dream is great and all, but when the adventure of pulling away, downsizing, building, learning off-grid technology, applying it, adjusting habits, and making a home out of the new place is under control, what you have left is just *keeping it real*.

"We are a team," he said. I felt it. We always are.

Besides, I thought, *what better things do I have to do with my time?*

1. Knees
February 25, 2016

It was Mike's birthday and we decided we wanted to go downhill skiing to celebrate. We scanned the calendar and decided to go on the Tuesday after Presidents' Day Vacation. While the rest of the world would be snuggling back into their routines of work and study, we reasoned, we would be free to enjoy having the slopes to ourselves. We checked the weather and ticket prices on line and picked what looked to be the perfect day.

Getting ready for any kind of trip involves a little cooking. Mike wanted bear pot pie instead of a cake. That would be easy, since we canned up a *shitton* of bear last fall. I also made up some scones and bought some grape tomatoes and oranges from the store. Oh, yeah, and we had to gather up our equipment. I didn't have any problem locating ski pants, hats, gloves, and long underwear because we use them all of the time up here. The helmets, goggles, skis and poles were all in the basement stacked not-so-neatly behind other stuff we knew we'd use again someday.

We left before dawn. The Hunger Moon was rising majestically over the tree-lined mountains and Nature decided to accentuate her pearly glory with a pink lens. We watched it with gratitude; drank hot coffee and ate our buttery scones.

"What's our middle name?" Mike was setting me up for our little skit.

"Adventure!" I answered with a fisted right arm leaning forward like a good actress who had rehearsed her lines to the point of believing she is the character. The only difference is that I really *am* that character and she's writing the script.

"Yahoo!!!"

It was the first time in a while that we had been able to cut loose and do something a little irresponsible that cost some money. I didn't realize how long a while it had been until we checked in and got our lift tickets.

We had never skied Sugarloaf Mountain before so we joked around with the young woman at the counter and tried to get the scoop before heading out. The last thing you want to do is get on the wrong lift that takes you way up to the top of a mountain and you only have double black diamond trails to choose from for your descent. A perfect day could get ugly fast.

"How long has it been since you last skied?" Our attendant was being pleasant and capable.

"Let's see." I reached into the pocket of my ski jacket where I usually keep the last lift ticket. *February 14, 2009.* "Yeah, um…not since the year our eldest daughter graduated from high school. That tells you a few things, doesn't it?"

We all laughed since she looked like she was still in college or was the age when you're just working to keep up with your loans.

"Yes, well, you might want to start on the bunny slope over here," she indicated a small lift and section at the base of the mountain that you could call the *slush fund.*

We thanked her and followed a school of tiny green-neon ski jackets, adorable pink pom-pommed helmets, and an enchanting tot wearing the smartest glittery purple tutu I have ever seen.

Second and third-graders may seem heartwarmingly cute and cuddly but, like puppies, they can tear things up in minutes. These little munchkins are absolutely fearless. They have no regard for the sensible folk next to them diligently practicing their pie-slices and leaving behind rust tracks reminiscent of pizza-grease.

I couldn't keep my mind from going back to that old lift ticket. *Wow! Seven years! Biologically speaking, a person is completely different in seven years. Any cell in my body that might have remembered how to swoosh down a mountain gracefully has long since met its fate.* Needless to say, my confidence wavered a bit. But somehow, somewhere, between head, arms, and legs, some written record must have been passed down from one cell generation to the next. A recipe called "How to Swoosh" must have survived the flood of seven years because I was still able.

Mike's brain works more in cartoons. He's just like the Roadrunner. "Come on, let's take the quad up to the top of the mountain!"

"Well, maybe we should start in steps. Take it slow, you know…" So we did. Let's face it, the only reason why he can still walk is because he keeps chasing Bugs Bunny. *Or is that why he keeps getting hit by the oncoming train?*

As it turns out, safety does kill because the last thing you can do when you're heading downhill on two slippery boards over icy patches is to try and take it slow. So that's how I fell and twisted my left knee. I wasn't worried. It reminded me that I had to lift with my heart center, align my hips and shoulders, use both feet (think about activating the outer edges), and smile.

It was an amazing day and I got a spectacular picture of Mike on the summit with snowy mountain ranges behind him. We ate bear pie for lunch in the base lodge and stopped mid-afternoon for a hot chocolate in one of the upper lodges. The sun was shining and the conditions were just perfect.

Skiing that day reminded me of my inner strength and taught me that life requires courage which can be best found by lifting your heart. Life requires that we are better off going with the flow rather than trying to slow it down or change it. What is required is that we look forward, not back. It is best if we are mindful of the people in front of us, not behind us. They will be able to take care of themselves if they do the same. Looking ahead, we scope out a safe out-of-the-way place to pause for our companions. We pay attention to the signs. We gratefully accept a stranger's helpful hand when we fall. We keep our skis facing downhill because any other direction is just unnatural.

We remember that at the end of the day, we all will end up in the base lodge, looking our worst with matted sweaty hair (if you still have some), walking around with that charming ski boot waddle, and ragingly chapped skin (some of us). We will all be incredibly happy to be warm, to be out of our impossible boots, feeling like we lost forty pounds, and content we made it.

The adorable little skiers, like a collection of jelly beans, are back to being sweet and cute while their parents attend to their needs. It's great to watch from a distance but I'm kind of glad I'm not on my knees, unstrapping an expensive pair of boots that will have to be replaced before they're even scratched up. I do, nevertheless, applaud the immense efforts those parents are making to teach their kids how to downhill ski. Ultimately, it is a good thing to know how to do. Like learning how to golf, it teaches a certain etiquette and civility.

Admittedly, like golf, it takes up a lot of room. Ski resorts do cut through natural habitats in a large way. They also, however, attract people to appreciate the wilderness on their own terms. It's a survival strategy. Even those people we know that approach nature from the most primitive vantage point, still rely on human trappings of some sort to survive out there.

When I see people on the ski slopes, I see people who are exposing themselves to the hazards of nature. The first of these is gravity. Whether you manage to make it down gracefully on polished skiis or you are helped down by a ski patrol gurney, you're getting down that mountain. The second is the cold. The world as we know it is run primarily by folks who sit in controlled temperatures all day and go home to a controlled temperature. For most people, it takes some buffing up of the skin to consider minus ten degrees and forty mile-an-hour winds a fun time. It helps to have good outerwear made by other folks who work in controlled temperature environments (we hope, anyway).

Like all species, humans are programmed to survive. They want their danger to be controlled. They want calculated risks. Even our friends who live in earth shelters through the winters of Maine have a tool box of skills they have learned and honed in order to survive. If you think of it, their cells have acquired the information from the cells of others. Like all other organisms, we share survival information. The internet helps speed this up a little. It's a giant metaphor for the web of existence we all share and it can bring us all a little closer to Nature, if we are willing.

It is a lot like being on that ski slope. You're glad you have the equipment. It is true that people used to do it on handmade wooden boards. Our friend, Quimbly, used to ski on them with her Swedish father. They used leather straps to fasten them. It can be done. It requires practice. But somehow, I think it still required that her father spend some extended time down in their basement with wood, a planer, and beeswax. He learned how to do it from his father. Her mother was upstairs baking a pot pie she could pack up for lunch. Somehow, I can picture Quimbly's two parents dressed in canvas pants, on their knees, strapping leather ties on four sets of leather boots that would have to be replaced in a year.

We're really not that different, though the world is.

In spite of the exhilaration we get when we go on an adventure, trying something new and a little dangerous, it becomes really fun when our traveling becomes more familiar. The first time Mike and I made it down a new trail on our "new" mountain, we felt good. The subsequent times, we swooshed down gracefully and felt the rush of wind pass through our helmets, like the sounds of ancestors ringing in our ears, shouting "Yeah, baby!"

Of course, every adventure leaves a little mark. This time, it was my left knee. Since I was able to ski all day on it, I knew it wasn't seriously injured, but it definitely was sore when I finally took off my boots.

"Let's not wait another seven years before we do this again." Mike agreed. His legs were feeling it too. My knee was a reminder to me to keep on going. We had done what it takes to get to the place where we could play more. We had reared our children, planned, saved, studied, built, and created a means to make a living. We had sacrificed the controlled temperature environments and much of the daily equipment of comfort for the chance to live like this.

"Yes," I said, "Let's not wait too long between adventures. I have a story to write and it can't be about boring characters."

BEAR POT PIE

Up until the advent of the world's largest cinnabun (see chapter 22), Mike would rather have a pot pie than just about anything on his birthday. Even though it's never a surprise, I try to hide the fact that I have made one for him to surprise him anyway. When we have an adventure like skiing on his birthday, I have to be especially creative to hide a pot pie from him, especially if I want it to be warm when I give him a slice. Sometimes they may end up being hand-pies (kind of like large empanadas-same idea, anyway).

So here's the recipe. We start with pressure canning our bear. It makes the meat really tender and not gamey in any way. It also makes it very easy to make a pot pie. If you don't happen to have bear in your pantry, any manner of filling will do, of course.

The pie crust is best if you can use bear fat for it. It comes out light (believe it or not) and at the same time, nutritious. Bear fat is said to contain the highest concentration of vitamin D anywhere in nature. It makes sense since bears tend to hibernate or become very lethargic in the winter so they must survive off of their stored energy.

For the record, we do not hunt bear but when people do, we are the glad recipients of whatever they do not want. Very often that is the fat.

For pie crust: 2 cups flour (we use some of our own ground flour from whole berries that we sprout and dry mixed with regular white flour), salt, 2/3 cup bear fat (or any fat – butter is good) 6 tablespoons cold water (more or less). Mix up, roll out.

For filling: I usually use a larger cast iron pan to sauté some onion and garlic with leeks, carrots, and whatever else you have on hand, add a tablespoon of flour, salt, pepper, and then add your potted meat (in our case, bear). Do not overcook, just let the mixture dry out a bit so it is not runny but not overly dry. If it is too runny, add some potatoes and allow them to steam up a bit in the mixture.

Line a deep dish pie plate with half of the pie crust, add the mixture, and then top it with the other half of the pie crust. Make sure to create some vents by cutting a nice heart shape or star with the pointy end of a knife so that steam can escape. Bake at 350 degrees for about 45-50 minutes or until the crust is a golden color.

2. Dirt Road
March 11, 2016

"Hang on, I'm passing through the *Russel Rapids*," Mike's voice was agitated and garbled by the jouncing of our little (and old) Honda. If there's a quirky way to put something, you can count on Mike to coin it. We were on our way to town and I had asked him a question. At the moment, he could only concentrate on driving since the curve around Russel's is preceded by a stretch of road that is more rut than road. It takes some navigating to keep your wheels on the road side of the rut.

We live on a dirt road. Actually, we live on a dirt road off of approximately five miles of dirt road in each direction. This simple fact connects to a series of other simple facts that affect us daily. For one thing, it doesn't much matter where a dirt road goes. For us it is the path to "out". But for most other people it is a travel destination. Some people travel our road just for the sake of going for a drive to see something other than human activity (some wildlife, perhaps, or just a beautiful river scene).

On a dirt road, we wave to each other because it is such a rarity to pass someone going in the other direction. It might not be much, but our simple, creatively maintained road is what we have. We could all go in to Town Hall and demand that our road be paved, but we all know that eventually it is just going to lead to higher taxes so most of us are resigned (if not content) to keep our dirt roads.

"I can save you a whole lot of time writing that chapter you say you're working on," said Lori from Town Hall. It was 9 a.m. on Wednesday morning and the office was full because it is only open from nine to eleven on Wednesdays and five to seven on Thursdays. But, if you call Marie with something you really need done, she'll open up for you. You might get a call yourself if the town needs something done, like the time Mike got a call to clear some fallen trees out of the road after a storm. We didn't mind because we got a good half cord of wood out of the "favor". It also keeps our taxes lower.

"Just make a photocopy of a piece of Swiss cheese," she said, "and place it right there in the book! That would explain everything." I thought about it.

There are a few more "rapids" on our road into town. I like to think of it as the road growing its own speed bumps. Those of us who live on the road know when to go slower and when to slow down. Even so, I have to admit, I have been guilty of speeding along our road to get somewhere in too little time. I always end up regretting it when I bottom out and the back-end slams into gravel. You know you are on a quality dirt road when you apologize to your car out loud.

When it gets like this, we don't get too many visitors. They tell you that you're just not worth the wear and tear on their cars (and fillings). It's not like this all of the time, just when the road freezes, thaws, and then freezes again. Or when there's a heavy rain. It's the pockets of water that do it. That's when you get some real class four rapids.

In the spring, the roads get flooded and it is pretty easy to misjudge how deep the water is. There's a certain point where it will carry your car downstream with you in it if you misjudge. Usually, our neighbors will let the Town Office know and they'll put signs up to close the road. But, sometimes, you have to gage that yourself.

That's what happened the day Mike had decided to give it a try in the Jeep. I went ahead in my tall rubber boots to indicate to him how deep the water was. You can't always go by other vehicles that make it through, even if you think you have more clearance than they do. It seemed alright, so I got back in. The problem is that rivers can rise faster than you think.

I was watching the water level rise as Mike drove the Jeep slowly through the water. Keep in mind here that it was going to tack on a little over an hour to take the other way around through a neighboring town.

"Mikey, I don't think we should keep going." I was detecting a change in the water level since I was able to look out of the window as he crept along.

"Don't worry. We'll make it." I usually defer to Mike's spatial intelligence when it comes to these sorts of things. My sense of what fits where or how much something can hold isn't usually as accurate as his. But this was a case of more space than intelligence.

"Uh, hon…" I had opened the Jeep door and could see the water just below the running boards. "This thing is about to float…"

"Naw…we're almost past the high stuff…"

I was getting out. I had seen the You-Tube videos. You know the ones. It's where the guy driving thinks it isn't as deep as it is and he's almost at the end of it.

"What are you doing?"

"I'm getting out. If you want to go canoeing down river in this Jeep, by all means go for it…but I'm not going with you." My voice was calm and matter-of-fact. That's what did it for him. He finally took his eyes off of the "road" and saw how deep the water had really gotten. I'm not bragging, but I'm pretty sure I saved both of us and the Jeep that day. There was just enough clearance for him to keep contact with the road and turn around.

That's how our road gets sometimes. Other times it will be so dry that you're glad you don't live too close to it or that you're not travelling it by foot when the huge logging trucks tear through. The dusting is impressive. It coats your windows and you can only imagine what it does to your lungs. That's when the Town Hall sends out a truck with a big water tank to hold the road together before it all blows away.

Most of the time, however, our road is just beautiful. In the winter we'll be lucky to pass one car or truck and if it's not one we recognize, we wonder who it is and where they're going. In the summer, we can't keep track but we know the people in those cars are visiting the camps we have all along the rivers and lakes in this region. Their cars are just too new looking.

Occasionally, we'll see someone by the side of the road, fixing a flat or some other thing. That's how we met our neighbors Anne and Phil. She had a flat and four little kids in the car. He met her in his truck to fix her flat tire. It was steaming hot and she had stopped right by the bog where the mosquitoes were so thick we were breathing them in. Mike and I stopped.

On a regular road, you might have seen that Anne had plenty of able help. On a regular road, Phil might have rejected the help, saying he had it all under control. But I don't care how used to mosquitoes you are, you never have much under control when you're in the middle of a swarm.

"At least I can help you get out of here faster," Mike said. And that was the case. It was also the beginning of a neighborly relationship.

Our road goes to nowhere. We know it, but it's everything we need. We have a pretty close relationship with that road. Some of us stop and pick up bits of garbage. We stop our trucks and visit with neighbors on that road. If you pull to the side, we'll probably slow down, roll down the window, and ask you if everything is alright. It doesn't matter if you are a young man, or a couple with everything under control. The next person down that road will probably stop and check on you.

We might also pull over to see what the bald eagle is up to, if the ice is melting, the river rising, or the moose out grazing. We might just stop to see if the fiddlehead ferns are sprouting or where the elderberries will be found.

You can usually tell who lives on a dirt road when you see them. Their cars and trucks are covered in dust. There's no point in cleaning a car that travels down a dirt road daily. By the time you get back home from town or to town from home, you're completely dusted again. What's the point of that?

One of the good things about mud season is that your car doesn't get filled with dust but the interior will get dirty as you and your dog will track in some mud. It's just the way it is because chances are your driveway is a gravelly dirt road too. Few people on our road have paved driveways. In fact, I can't think of any, at the moment.

There's something impermanent about a dirt road. It's almost as though we remember that we are borrowing this space from Nature. We haven't just commandeered the space to never return it again like most roads do. If we left our road for just a few seasons, it would be crowded in by Nature's creations.

Our road still belongs to Nature and she takes over sometimes. That happened the time our friends were visiting. They are a new couple, still in that lovey-dovey stage. It was really fun spending time with them as they rekindled that lovey-dovey thing in us. Right now Mike would say that the world is his sandbox because when we decided to go into town in separate cars, we were delayed by a spectacular sight.

First it was a bull moose who was taking his time to cross the road in front of us. It took him so long that our friends pulled their car alongside of ours. We could have been watching a drive-in movie. The large male was eventually followed by a cow who sauntered prettily across the road. He had been waiting for her and they took their time, as though to say, "Look, we're frisky and lovey-dovey too!"

There are so many things to see along our road. You might see a hand-painted sign asking residents to help out at the grange since there's a group of us drywalling and painting on Saturday mornings in the spring. For those of us who live on that road, the sign of hope is a blaze orange placard posted on trees and poles along the road telling the trucks to avoid usage because it is too soft in the spring. It is almost as welcome a sight as the daffodils that pop up as our hopeful sign that winter is finally, well almost finally, over. Blaze Orange is the first sign of spring.

I would like to post a sign myself. It would say:

To those who travel down our road, please slow down and enjoy the view.

Wave if someone waves to you. You might not know who they are but then again, you might, and then will regret it if you passed them without saying hello.

Remember that traveling with your tailgate down is no way to clean out a truck.

One of us, passing you in an old dusty truck will end up picking up your junk if you do.

That's no way to say thank you to folks who manage to keep a dirt road going.

FLUID FILMING

There are a lot of things that must be done to keep our vehicles in good running order. One of those things is to mitigate some of the damage that our cars are going to incur on our road, mostly in the other three seasons of the year. When you live on a dirt road, the biggest problem is all of the calcium chloride that the town sprays to keep the dust down. That is the kind of stuff that just eats a vehicle's frame.

So one of the things that Mike does is he fluid films the undersides of our vehicles in the fall and in the spring. This ensures that the dirt will stick to the fluid film and create a thick layer of protection on the frame.

One of the tricks is that before you fluid film the underside of your car, you have to wash off any of the dirt that is already on the frame. The best and easiest way to do it is to take a cheap deck scrubber for a power washer, flip it upside down and strap it to the base of an old office chair. Move that rolling base up and down under the car so that you get the entire underside of the car without even getting wet.

Then, use a paint sprayer with a compressor or use a spray bottle and just start squirting. You cover everything. Some people use their used motor oil from an oil change (not the best for the environment). Fluid film is lanolin. If you manage to get some on your hands, it could make your skin happy.

3. Small
September 30, 2016

I went and did it. I got a job. It's not just any job. It is teaching Spanish in the secondary school in my closest town. In order to stay open, our high school houses fifth grade through twelfth grade and its population is under 500 students.

I've never officially taught Spanish (other than some tutoring because I speak it). At the moment, I'm not certified to teach Spanish. But I am a certified English teacher. So when I heard that our local school really needed a Spanish teacher, I applied for the job and got it.

I have a short commute to work and I couldn't be happier. I'm also bringing in a paycheck. With the way our car situation was going last winter, I figured it was about time I started to put my skills and experience to good use so I started thinking about what jobs I could do to bring in a little more money.

I had considered magazine writing, working on a farm, increasing my yoga schedule, working more with Mike, and other stuff. I was getting pretty consistent work as a sub but it's not the best income generator and has all of the downsides of teaching with few of the benefits.

So when the door opened, it seemed pretty clear that I needed to walk through it and apply for the teaching job. You might ask why they would hire a Spanish teacher on a provisional certification. It is because by August 15th, with a state mandated Foreign Language graduation requirement looming overhead, they were getting desperate. For me, that meant that the door was wide open. It also meant that I had to really believe that I could do it and prove it.

My new job has meant some study and a lot of creative planning. I had forgotten (if I ever even knew) where all of the accents go, what odd nouns should be masculine or feminine, and the names of all the verb tenses. My Spanish is a good working Spanish. It comes naturally and I have a good accent but it requires a little polishing if I'm going to teach it to others.

So, I have been studying and planning non-stop for the last few months. But, my students have been so helpful and eager to learn, that it hardly seems like work. Our school is so small that I have Spanish I, III, and Spanish for Spanish speakers all in one class. That's what I call specialized learning. But my class sizes are small enough that I actually can do it.

In a small school, every student counts. Every athlete plays pretty much every sport. At pep rallies, the band stops playing when the athletes are on the court being introduced because most of the band seats are empty. In a small school like this, we can still host a bonfire after the homecoming parade because half of the town shows up. We don't worry about needing enough chaperones.

So what's the size of the graduating class in a school like this? This year it will be twenty-eight, if they all make it. In its heyday, it was sixty-seven. Many of my colleagues are graduates of the school. There's history here. Deep history. Many teachers married their high school sweethearts. Funny thing is, they are still married to them. Some of their children are teachers here. I like the simplicity of that, the comfort of knowing that your school is full of families and it is a place where you belong.

I'm not saying that our school doesn't have its share of drama and angst. Those things pervade even the most guarded places. Girls and boys can be really off-putting if they haven't yet experienced what's it's like to be put off. It's human nature to feel better than others. It actually is built into our psyches to seek that feeling in order to increase serotonin.

The truth is, when people of all ages feel insecure, they usually try to counter it by appearing to be really tough. True grit is the person who can smile in the face of judgement. The one who can be genuinely courteous to someone new who might have averse opinions is the one who is really tough. Being charming is disarming.

What I try to teach my kids in small increments is that believing in yourself is the best way to kick off a good serotonin rush. As it turns out, being *trustworthy* happens to be another solid way to increase that happy brain chemical. Trusting in yourself to take the higher road in interpersonal relationships can give you a supersized burst of that feel-good chemical and is a healthy addiction.

Many times we who work in schools get frustrated by the fact that a kid can get through eleven years of school and then drop out a few months from the finish line. It is a hard thing to watch. Nobody has a better frontline view of the insanity of this phenomena like the office secretaries.

"I try to tell the kids who get signed out by their parents that they need to be here, get through, and move on. But they don't seem to care," Janet tells me. I sense the frustration in her voice. As much as teachers and school personnel would like to influence kids to do the right thing, the ultimate authority figure is still the parent.

In a small town like this one, it doesn't take long to get the backstory on some families. It isn't always pretty.

But like our kids, we can either feel powerless to change circumstances, or we can accept that whatever changes we can make will be small ones.

A series of small changes can add up. I like to remind myself that it starts with small things like a genuine smile or eye contact. Sometimes it is a kindly spoken word of truth. It could be a mindfully phrased lesson about interpersonal skills like saying hello to people when you see them or thanking them when they come to see you play softball. Other times, it could be as subtle as just being who you are and modeling the fact that your life might not be perfect and totally in control but you are happy with who you are.

I ask myself why I chose to go back into the fray when I could just as easily have stayed home in my peaceful little spot by the river and written tributes to nature. I don't know for sure what the answer is but I think it has to do with keeping it real. It has to do with participating in this thing we call life.

It has to do with the 'A' student who comes from a really tough background, who can't afford to go to the next town's "public/private" school. It is about the families who strive to make good choices, who struggle to ground their kids while holding down two jobs to make ends meet. My being present and providing an interesting classroom that exposes kids to other world views is a message to the kids who work hard to believe in themselves that someone cares about their struggle. It is an open door to a whole world out there of people just like us who are struggling in their own way.

It's not that I don't care about the ones who have given up, but I also care about the ones that have a fighting chance. To me, that's the real fight. It's the kids who are being neglected who still manage to find a reason to believe in themselves and come to school and dream of going to college and developing a career that I'm here for. It's the ones who were homeschooled and are back in for a broader education that I am here for. I'm here for the quiet ones, the ones who take instruments home and those who forgo Instagramming friends so they can practice their lines for the school play. I'm here for the ones who run during the summer to keep in shape for soccer. I'm here for the families that believe in their town and could send their kids to the public/private school in the next town, but don't.

The famous actress, Sarah Bernhardt, once said, "You must spend yourself in order to be rich."

Sarah clearly had a big attitude, spreading herself all over the place like that. But then again, she probably was one of those kids who walked home alone so she could practice her lines for the school play.

Teachers have a tendency to say things like, "You never know, the next Sarah Bernhardt could be sitting in my classroom right now." This is true. Sarah most surely sat in a little desk with her fountain pen and little lined notebook, taking down notes from a black chalkboard where some teacher, probably all worn around the edges, spent himself day after day in a peaceful monotone, believing that someday one of those little kids might be famous and he played a small part in it.

If I had a pocketful of coins I could spend, it would be on things like giving a kid a reason to want to be in school. It would be on teaching kids who Sarah Bernhardt was. It would be spent on challenging kids to stretch and grow. It would be spent to encourage a kid to fundraise for two years so he/she could travel to Central America for ten days on a school trip. I would spend all of my wealth on listening to kids, looking them in the eyes, and telling them that I care, that I too have seen tough times but have survived just fine because I believed in myself.

Though having a job is ultimately about bettering one's income, what I am gaining has a lot more to do with what I'm spending. Admittedly, what I have in my pocket right now still isn't a whole lot. It's just some small change.

TORTILLAS

One of the things I like to do is show my students how to cook real food. As a Spanish teacher, I know that it is common to teach kids how to make sweet treats like churros and flan but I like to show my kids how to make things that are practical and good for them.

One of those things is tortillas. Here are a few reasons why a kid in Maine might want to know how to make a tortilla from scratch. First, it is one of the cheapest high-protein foods you can make with limited cooking supplies. Two, it is a food that is versatile. It can be eaten with a little oil and salt, butter, cheese if you have some, or anything else you have on hand. Three, it is a whole grain food that is low in fat. Four, it teaches students how the indigenous peoples from Central and South America treat the corn so that the body can absorb its nutrients.

Tortilla mixes can be found in almost any grocery store. It costs about $2.47 for a five pound bag. The bag will make up to nine pounds of tortillas. That's a lot of tortillas!

To make them, you mix two cups of your tortilla mix (Maseca) with one-and-a-half cups warm water, a little salt and mix with you hand until it feels like playdough. Take a ball a little larger than a golf ball on your cupped palm and roll it into a smooth ball. You take a ziplock bag or any plastic bag and cut it so that it will cover the top and bottom of your tortilla when you flatten it. I showed them how you can use a medium or small cast-iron pan to smoosh it down evenly until you have a flat patty. Cook it without oil in any pan you would like. It can be a fat free food that way. Turn it a few times. There you have it! When they are fresh, you can eat them just as they are with no toppings.

As far as their being made of corn and being nutritious, there is a trick to how you make corn actually digestible. (Kids make funny observations about corn and the human digestion and they are right!) However, the indigenous peoples of the Americas have known for thousands of years that corn is a wonderfully nutritious grain but it must be soaked in the naturally occurring mineral, lime, which is a base and breaks down the grain so that the human body can absorb its nutrients. That is why tortillas taste so good to us, especially when they are homemade. Oh yeah, did I mention that they are gluten-free? Yup, that too! Delicioso.

3. Junk
November 3, 2016

My parents are visiting next week and there's a lot of what they would call junk in the yard. Since they live in a suburban South Florida town, I know their tolerance for junk in the yard is pretty slim. You might even say that when they visit us, they have to try really hard not to be intolerant of stuff in the yard that they don't quite understand. Like Mike's old Honda.

Or, for instance, the old compressor that Mike rescued from somewhere. Most people would think, what good is that old bulky and rusty engine that is just sitting out in the rain? My answer is, I have no idea, but I know Mike does.

That man can fix anything, as long as he has access to a butter knife. Well, the truth is, when you are the one fixing all of your tools, you need a lot of tools. You also need a good supply of junk at hand that could be used to fix stuff. I'm pretty sure that an old engine is in that category of useful junk.

Conversations around these parts might start with a "Hey, how're you doing?" but eventually, it's going to end up with someone telling the story of how they were able to use some piece of junk to solve a problem.

Then there's the conversation about how much time a person spends bundling it up into little parcels under camo tarps and behind sheds. That's usually a wife talking. In fact, having a place to store junk is one good reason to have a shed. It's not because you're putting your junk into the shed (there's obviously not enough room for that stuff). It is so that you have a buffer zone that keeps the stacked up stuff out of view.

Winter is perfect for people up here because at least half of the year you never even know you have that much junk. The downside is, if you are looking for something, you'd better know you need it before winter comes in November because you'll never find it under the ice and snow layers later on.

That can happen to tools of any function if you have not put them away in the fall. You never know when the stuff-hiding snow is going to pack your stuff up for the winter. Of course, spring is a great time of discovery. It can also be really disappointing when you discover that the very thing you've been looking for all winter spent the past seven months only a few feet from the back door.

Once winter takes its coat off, nature finds itself in its birthday suit and everything just feels a little vulnerable. That's true of our junk too. We start to see it for what it is.

To an inventor, it is potential. To some, it represents a little human fear. We are expecting that whatever it is we own is going to break someday. We expect that we are going to need to fix something, or revive something that worked once and we might need again. We are never really sure what the future will bring but we feel pretty confident that some of it might include breakage so we do our best to prepare for that eventuality. That's the kind of fear that makes us hold on to our junk.

Either of these could have been the reason that our neighbor held on to the top of a galvanized garbage can after he rolled over the can itself with his car. The incident happened probably about ten years ago but he was glad he had kept that lid.

It came in handy when he was hired to create an exhaust system for my friend Lyn's new pottery kiln. He fabricated an entire system out of the junk in his yard. His kit consisted of an old propane tank, some aluminum flange material, some metal rebar, and his treasured garbage can lid to keep the rain out of the vent system. There you have it. With some accomplished welding skills, you end up with a substantial solution to venting Lyn's high fire gas kiln. Problem solved.

Most people in Maine either store junk or have been the beneficiary of other people's junk. The sign of a close friend is when a person allows you to go through their junk to find something you might need. So many times Mike has said he can fix something. When I ask what he's going to do he'll say, "I don't know, I haven't looked through my *junque* yet." (He says his junk is spelled that way.)

Metal junk is especially valuable around here. Mike salvaged a stainless steel countertop from volunteering a month of Saturdays for a restore we did at the town hall last spring. So far he has used it to create a stainless steel cooktop for our woodstove that I absolutely love. It can be quite a business if you're willing to pick up and haul away other people's eyesores. That's how we finally got rid of the plow that was attached to our truck that burnt down a few winters ago. I saw someone in a small pick-up truck picking through our neighbor's trash for metal junk one day and asked him if he wanted the plow.

For those of you who have the benefit of living in warmer climates (that's just about everyone, I think), a plow is the heavy metal thing you attach to the front of your truck to shovel away all of that snow you get up here. Almost everybody owns one if they live any distance from the main road. It is usually a rusty old truck that isn't really road worthy because if it is, it won't be for very long. It gets pretty beat up from the act of ramming snow into eight foot banks of ice.

The junk-picker asked if he could come back later and I told him no problem. I assumed he needed to come back with a friend and a bigger truck since the plow probably weighs about as much as his small pick-up. Nope.

He had taken the time to empty out the bed of his truck and came back by himself. Fortunately, Mike was home when he returned because he did need a little help using a couple of saved-up pressure treated two-by-sixes to get some leverage under the plow. Mike stood the plow on end and let the guy back into it and it fell into his truck bed.

Somehow they managed to get that plow enough into the picker's truck and somehow the picker was able to drive his truck where he needed to go without getting stopped by the Sheriff. When he drove off, I was thinking I would believe more in traveling by magic carpet than in that truck. The picker was smiling ear-to-ear with a plow chucked half-way into the bed of his little pick-up with front tires that barely touched ground.

If he could find a way to get that plow home, working again, and freshly painted, he might be able to resell it for close to $800. We couldn't help thinking that he deserved it and were glad that we made him so happy. We were also glad to get a clear spot back in the yard.

And so it is with junk. The bottom line is it makes a man happy. I'm not so sure about how womenfolk might feel about it most of the time. It does tend to be a good collecting place for mosquito larvae and mouse nests. But the way I look at it is, if it can cause Mike a little pleasure to pick through his *junque* and find just the part he needs to get that blade trimmer going again, maybe he can trim the tall grass around that pile by the shed this summer.

That might neaten things up a little for my parents' visit. Then everyone is happy.

BOLOS LEVEDOS

One of the things that Mike loves is when I make these little round and sweet Portuguese breads that his grandmother would make for him. I cheat a little because frankly, I am just not that good at making dough rise so I use my bread machine to make the dough. I can hear grandma telling me that it is fine. According to Mike, she was like that. As long as it makes him happy, who cares how you do it, she probably would say. Since I started teaching again, there is a bit of a gap between the things I would like to do and the things I actually have time to do.

So, here is why I make bolos (pronounced *bool* – like fool with a b) for Mike. It is an extremely versatile little bread that can be used to make sandwiches but can also be eaten just as is, with a little butter, a fried egg, some cheese, if you want. That way, he can throw together a lunch very easily before leaving in the morning.

Another reason why I love these little breads is that you DO NOT HAVE TO BAKE THEM! You cook them on a griddle on top of the stove with no oil so clean-up is easy. They are so easy to make because of that. For those of us who live off grid, using the oven, even though it is gas, can use a lot of power because of the glow plug so whatever I can do on the stovetop, is helpful, especially in the winter.

One more reason to love these little breads is that I get to use that new custom-made stainless steel cook top to "bake" the bolos on the woodstove.

Keep in mind that these are sweet breads and they are quite rich. But that is what makes them so great.

So here's the recipe:

Dissolve 2 teaspoons yeast in ¼ cup warm water and a pinch of sugar. Set it in a warm place to activate the yeast for 10 minutes (this is a key step so don't skip it, trust me).

Put the following wet ingredients in a large bowl (or your breadmaker).

3 eggs
¼ cup melted butter, cooled
½ teaspoon salt
1 ¼ cups milk

Add the following dry ingredients
6 cups all-purpose flour (you can mix your own)
1 cup white sugar

Add the yeast sponge and knead until smooth (about 10 minutes). If you are using your breadmaker, set it for dough. Mine takes about an hour and a half and draws very little power because it doesn't bake the bread.

If you are doing it by hand: lightly cover it and set the dough aside in a warm spot until it doubles (45 minutes).

Here is where we come together again. When your dough is ready, cut it into 15-20 pieces of equal size and then roll each one into a ball and flatten with the palm of your hand. Set on a baking sheet that is dusted with corn meal, dust both sides. Cover and let rise (could take up to an hour – I'm not always that patient). Cook on your stovetop griddle surface until both sides are golden brown. You have to let them rest for a good 10 minutes before eating or they will be gooey and uncooked inside. Just for the record, Mike always eats them when they are gooey like that and says that's when they are their best. *A little butta'*…you get the idea. "Rico" is the same in Spanish and Portuguese.

5. Purpose
December 11, 2016

It is Sunday. There might be a snow day tomorrow. Then again, there might not be. The temperature outside is 4 degrees and I slept like a little baby in her mother's arms last night. I sleep that way because the woods hold me in a warm embrace.

The wood stove did its job very well last night and the first thing I did this morning was to put on a pot of coffee and stoke up the dark stove. The prospect of a quick fire seemed a bit dim. To get the stove lit again might require a trip outside for several categories of kindling and fire-starting materials which include, but are not limited to, newspapers, birch bark, chips of cedar from our house-building, and thin pine kindling that Mike set up on the covered deck. I just wasn't dressed for that yet.

Fortunately, with a little consistent puff-puffery of the bellows, I was able to get the coals to spark up a little life. With a few pages of newspaper and scraps of other fire starting materials I had on hand, I had a roaring fire going in less than an hour.

It was pre-dawn. Every bit of my focus was on stoking up that fire. I couldn't have been happier. The fire brought out my full gratitude since it required that I do nothing but tend to its needs. I can think of no other thing, except perhaps listening to a child, that requires full, undivided attention like making a fire.

It might seem a bit pagan but I think of it more as human to take the time to be grateful for the power that made it possible for man to create fire. However humans stumbled upon or were given the ability to make fire, it is a humbling experience to bow before some darkened coals buried in ashes and have the faith that with some human intention, those coals will come alive.

While teaching again has made these fire-stoking experiences a lesser part of my routine and more of Mike's routine, the beauty of tending the fire has not been lost to me. The connections are clear in my mind. I have been tending to another hearth, my own hearth. I have fanned up the flames of my soul and have renewed my purpose.

My mind still weaves the poetry as I approach the dark coals. I see myself in those coals. I am made of the same stuff as wood. I systematically add layers of growth around me. My limbs stretch outward, finding the support of nothing but air. They reach, nevertheless, supported by a spiraling action and refusing to succumb to gravity. Each day my roots seek the cool, damp minerals of unleavened matter and in doing so, add air to spaces that would otherwise be hard-packed.

This morning's fire awarded me the opportunity to focus every living breath to *its* purpose, reminding me that in spending myself, I am by nature, getting lighter. Ashes to ashes, my mind wanders. There is beauty in becoming ash. I would never want to leave myself as a piece of charred oak, for example. There is in that, a usefulness that never found its purpose.

Tending the fire teaches me that I can regain that same awareness in a place like school where, by nature, we are all multi-tasking all of the time. When, in the company of that chaos, I can find the presence of mind to focus all of my attention on a child when she speaks to me, I am in touch with purpose.

While there is value in imparting knowledge as a teacher, I also know that my purpose there runs deeper than simply knowledge. Learning another language and about other cultures is imminently valuable. But listening to a child might be even more so.

Today's lesson, I think, is about spending myself. It is about living the message that life is tough, but when we dig deep and learn how to spend whatever it is we have, whether it be given to us or through the scrapings of whatever small kindling we could muster up, we can keep our hearths burning brightly; and when life dampens our coals a little, it might take some effort and all of our focus, but we can always muster up a little human intention to make our soul fires burn again.

ELDERBERRY SYRUP

Elderberries grow wild around these parts so collecting the little dark purple berries with a mighty purpose in the winter is easy, once you can identify where they are. This plant is sometimes called ditch berry because it likes to plant itself in the ditches on the sides of roads. That also means that when the towns come around to cut back the growth along the sides of the roads, they either duck back into the thickets or get wacked.

So, that is why I planted an elderberry bush in our back yard close to our chicken coop. I figured that the bush would provide the birds some shade, protection from areal predators like the local bald eagle, and food when some of the riper berries fall.

I still collect berries when they ripen out in the wild but my home plant tells me when they will be ripe. It also tells me when to look for the bunches of little white blossoms that fan out from a center stem in the summer. Since elderberry plants like to grow in thickets with other plants, it can be difficult to see them once the flowers turn to berries. That is why it is best to spot the plants when the flowers are in bloom.

I know quite a few people living in the temperate zone who buy elderberry tablets at the pharmacy or health food store to boost their immune systems during flu season. I believe that the syrup is far superior to capsules and is even more so if you make your own syrup from fresh berries. All you need is elderberry and sugar. I know it sounds counterintuitive to put white sugar into something that is meant to boost your immune system but, by golly, it works.

I have tried to minimize the amount of sugar I used and my elderberry syrup was turning into elderberry wine even while in the refrigerator. If that sounds like a good plan, that is fine. Just remember that when you ferment any alcohol, it is best to allow air to escape but not enter the bottle. Otherwise, if you tap it up too tight, the gases that the fermentation process releases has nowhere to go and the pressure can build up to a point where the bottle blows. That probably would not happen in the fridge since the cold slows down fermentation. It is just something to think about if you plan to cut back on sugar.

We have talked about using honey to make our elderberry syrup. The only problem with that method is that elderberries must be heated to release their flavor and healthful benefits. Heating the honey will kill its natural enzymes and render it useless as an immune booster. So that is why I still use plain white sugar to make my elderberry syrup. But, I invite you to experiment on your own and come up with your own recipe because it is one of the best things you can do to stave off sickness and recover faster. Honest.

So, here's my recipe. Take about five quarts of elderberries and put them in a stainless steel pot. Do not use aluminum because it will pit it and I'm not sure what the chemical process is but it doesn't sound like a good thing. Also, avoid using enamel coated pots like Le Creuset because the berries leave a residue and will stain the enamel so deeply that it is hard to clean the pot afterwards. Stainless steel cleans up pretty easily. Place two cups of sugar in your pot and one cup water. Bring to a boil and simmer for fifteen minutes. Strain and bottle.

I usually pour my syrup into bottles with a narrow neck like maple syrup bottles or liquor bottles. Because of the high sugar content, you should be able to store the bottles in a cool dry place until winter. So far, I have used every last drop of elderberry syrup I have made before the next summer. If you make a small batch or have room in your fridge, store it there.

P.S.- It tastes great on pancakes too!

6. Simplicity
January 21, 2017

As it turns out, the simple life isn't all that simple. There's so much to do when you live a simple life. Anybody who has ever tried it would say that living the complex life is a whole lot easier. It just isn't nearly as fun.

Take, for instance, my buddy Willie. She lives in an old farmhouse and still makes all of her own pie crusts. ("Why would you even ask?!" she'll reply if you query her on whether the crust is homemade on her latest Dutch Apple or Blueberry). She grows and cans all of her own veggies, and makes a lot of stuff by hand. Her husband Bucky has been struggling with his health for the past several years and together they keep the old farmhouse in tiptop shape.

Bucky does what he can and mostly what he shouldn't, if you ask Willie. But Willie is the one who climbs up on the roof when we have had a heavy snowfall. That's something, when you consider Willie is in her seventies.

I think it helps that she has been taking my yoga class for a few years now but the truth is, Willie is just a strong Maine woman. She has been plowing snow in the winter and soil in the summer her entire life. And most of it has been done with simple hand tools. Her hands are always busy and they show it.

It would take me a lifetime to try and learn everything Willie and Bucky could teach me about not only the womanly arts like quilt and basket-making, but also how to track a deer and find your way through the woods (if you have a compass). The funny thing is, she's always telling me how smart I am and will follow it up with, "I'm just not that smart." I have to laugh. Willie is definitely in the top ten of the smartest women I have ever met. As hard as I try, I can't remember what the names of all of the wildflowers are that we encounter along our paths and how to tell the difference between the various types of fir (not "fur") trees. It takes a lot of critical thinking skills to navigate the woods the way she does.

"A lot of people think you move up here and live the simple life and it's going to be easy," she told me last week. (I'm picturing it and thinking yeah, like camping and fishing and berry-picking are all fun until it's part of your survival- it is still fun, though!) But I get it.

"It's a lot of a hard work," and I have to agree. But there's something fresh about Willie that I think her lifestyle does for her. It is hard work, for sure. Helping Bucky keep the old farmhouse going takes some endurance, but Willie spends a lot of time outside. If the woods were a church, Willie would be, hands down, the most pious person I have ever met.

When you keep an old farmhouse going like Willie and Bucky do, your routine begins early in the morning. You get up and make a fire, first thing. Bucky likes the house really warm so the wood stove is going all day long through most of the year. Up until last year, they had to stack all of their wood and then keep the wood box filled. A wood box opens on two sides: one side is in the wood shed or summer kitchen and the other is in the winter kitchen. Last year they decided to put in a pellet stove so the wood box is filled with pellets now. The only thing is that they still have to stack the 13,000 pounds of pellets in the fall. That's a lot of forty pound bags.

Next thing up is you bake something. That could be anything from pies, cookies, cereal bars, and strudels. Whatever it is, it is fresh and usually full of her handpicked berries. By the end of the fall, Willie has stocked her freezer and cupboards with almost everything she will need to get the two of them through the year.

Then you make breakfast for Bucky and help him get ready for the day. Even though he might not see anyone but Willie all day, Bucky always showers, shaves, and gets dressed in a clean pair of jeans, a crisp flannel shirt, and his L.L. Bean suspenders. Some things about being a warden just never leave you.

About now, it is getting to the end of January and we had a snowstorm last night that was measured in feet (close to three in some areas). Add that amount to what already fell and that's a whole lot of snow. The season isn't even over yet. One thing is for sure, if you let that kind of snow build up, you're asking for disaster. That's what happened to the old bowling alley in Millinocket. Its roof just caved right in.

Today, Willie is clearing off her back deck again so that when she clears the roof again, she won't have to lift double the amount of snow because what is on the roof will end up on her deck. Keeping her deck clear is key, considering she knows she will have to do it again very soon. Bucky does his best. He cuts paths and clears the driveway with the snow blower. Before Bucky fell ill, snow removal used to be his job, and like most men up here, he takes it seriously. Willie, like most of the women in Maine, always helped out with the shovel but now their roles are reversed. When the snow gets really heavy, Bucky just can't do it all the way he used to and it frustrates him.

The key to this kind of work, Willie tells me, is to keep up with it. You don't want it to, well, *snowball*.

When I look at Bucky and Willie, I think that this lifestyle really does "take two" and even though they both pay a high price when Bucky spends the next week doubled over in pain from all of the snow removal. His pride will not allow it to be a one-woman job.

By the third week in February, like clockwork, Bucky will have commandeered the kitchen table with his notebooks, catalogs, and long plastic bins of seeds, all organized according to his own thinking. He is already laying out his plans for the garden. Every now and again, he will hand me a pamphlet from 1953 about companion planting or how to prune an apple tree. I read them but my eyes glaze over afterwards and I think, "I don't know if I have it in me to be a good gardener."

"What do you want me to order for you?" Bucky will ask me. I am unusually hesitant. I can picture Bucky out there on his tractor, all bent over, refusing a hat while tending to his garden. Forcing himself to get out there in the blazing sun (you never can believe how hot Maine gets in the summer!), while I am lazing around my house, letting the dishes pile up. It is just hard to accept that kind of offer.

"Delicata!" I tell him since he's not going to give up. I know him better than to think I'm going to hold out anyway. Then I rationalize. If he's going to plant squash, why not plant the most amazing squash the human mind ever decided to hybrid. It's got a perfectly balanced sweet and nutty flavor with a firm texture. You never have to peel it. You just slice and go! Even the seeds are good. It also is the prettiest darned vegetable you will ever lay eyes on and most people just use it for decoration on the Thanksgiving table. But, veteran Mainers don't usually plant it because it doesn't store well in the root cellar. They go for the acorns and turban types like buttercup.

"Isn't there anything else?" This time I can hold out because I really *can't* think of anything else. Besides, as they both know, when I help them weed their garden, I end up with a grocery bag full of weeds like purslane and plantain that will go into my salads. I also am the beneficiary of everything else they can't eat or process themselves. On top of that, I worked out a good trade with Willie. In the summer months, she pays for her yoga classes with squash, lettuce, tomatoes, and lots and lots of zucchini.

When I think about the lives they both lived, I am amazed. When you listen to Bucky talk about his childhood, he will tell you that when he was ten years old, he began working in the potato fields pulling out the kale. "I got fired from that job," he said once. He explained that it was because he was too young. "You had to be twelve," he said.

When he was sixteen, he helped the river drivers from the shore of the river with a long pole to keep the logs from getting caught up on the shore. He got this job because he was too young to work with the machinery; it was too dangerous, the managers told him. Weighing in at just over a hundred pounds, it was a good way for a family to feed less mouths at the dinner table. It was also a good way to teach a boy about courage.

I guess the lessons worked because he joined the armed forces during Korea. He was a paratrooper and like many in his battalion, he injured his back with too many jumps. When he came back from war, he got a degree in forestry but there weren't too many jobs at that time in his field so he became a game warden. At 6' tall and supported by the kind of backbone that line of work will give you, it's no wonder that Willie, a woman as lithe and free as a deer, fell for him. It is worth mentioning that Willie still loves her freedom and Bucky is still a man of courage.

The farmhouse Bucky and Willie live in is the house his great grandparents lived in. There is a room above the summer kitchen they call the ram pasture where the loggers would stay. At one time, bunks packed the upstairs with some room for seating areas and one good window at the gable end. This is where the loggers would warm up after a long day of digging out stumps in the five feet of snow in February or would cool off after a day of baiting black flies with their body heat in July. The only break they would get would be mud season since there's no way to twitch out trees during the melt. (A twitch is a bundle of trees a horse can pull out in one trip.)

The last time Willie and I went out snowshoeing through the woods, she lamented about more and more people posting their properties so it is getting harder to hunt. (Oops...I told her that we just posted our land, but our posts list Mike's phone number to call if you want to hunt there.) She also talked about how many people are putting up gates so you can't run your ATV's along the old trails anymore.

She told me that after the last big snowfall, her new seasonal neighbors posted on Facebook that they had to snowshoe in and then shovel their way into the house the night they arrived for school vacation. It took them two hours and they were soaked and chilled to the bone when they finally made it into their cold cabin. It must have taken hours for that camp to warm up just above freezing.

Willie went over there the next day to say that the next time that happens, they should knock on her door and stay with them and dig out in the morning. They claimed it was too late at night; they did not want to bother her. Up here we know that people do not mind that kind of bother because next time, they might need to bother you. It is not about inconvenience. Sometimes it is about survival.

Every year, as more and more gates go up, more and more trails are choked off and there's less and less wild access for my two friends who used to run free all over these parts for days and see no other humans.

"I understand. Not everybody is respectful and knows about how things should be done. My brother posted his land because some hunter from out of town shot his dog within 200 feet of his house. You only have thirteen acres; it is probably a good idea to post it," she said.

We talked about what the next few years might look like for her. Taking care of the old farmhouse is getting tougher and tougher for them both. They have put it up for sale a few times but no one has bought it. I think about the fact that when it does sell, it probably won't belong to someone in the family for the first time in generations. But it is not the kind of house you can pack up for the winter and come back to in the summer. You have to live in an old farmhouse. It is the kind of house that will die if it is neglected.

I know that years from now, they will probably move to the Portland area to be closer to their kids and grandchildren. I feel a little pre-nostalgia coming on even though I'm pretty sure we have a lot of years left together. Bucky's loss in mobility has only seemed to sharpen his intellect. He's not going anywhere fast.

I think about our country and how many men like Bucky there are left to teach us things we need to know.

These are men who have had to face life with courage, who have roamed freely. They have run through the wild to bathe in rivers and lakes that see no other human foot prints. They have carried a gun and never used it irresponsibly. They have worked hard and smart, raised families, and faced horrors that haunt them still. They rail at the news, laugh at our jokes, and are always willing to teach what they know.

My pre-nostalgia turns romantic, and I think, yes, when the time comes, a young family will buy Bucky's ancestral farmhouse and will send their kids out to shovel the roof. The kids will put on their ski pants and relish the task since they will be able to slide off the roof of the woodshed into a seven foot bank of soft snow. They will have snowball fights and make snowmen that wave hi to the logging trucks as they zoom by.

Just like a person, when a house gets old, its spirit gets even more concentrated. With just a little attention, it possesses a certain pride that gives everyone who passes by a sense of tranquility and ease. An old house reminds us that this life and all of the things we think are so important right now, really are important and always have been.

Living in an old farmhouse is a living history lesson. You learn how to plant a summer garden, tend the blueberries, and how to prune the apple trees because you have to. Living that way makes you smarter since you already know how things used to be done and you are forced to figure out how things could be done better. You learn how to keep things going, how to manage your firewood, repair shingles, and floorboards, what kinds of squashes store best in your root cellar, how to keep your carrots in sand in the old crocks down there next to the rock foundation. You get to wonder what some of that stuff was used for down-cellar. Whether it is spending time with Willie in the woods or following Bucky around their old house, being with them is always an exercise in critical thinking.

The more I think about it, the more I realize that this kind of simplicity is pretty complex.

WILLIE'S FAMOUS PIE CRUST

When you ask Willie for a recipe she most likely won't need to consult her recipe book. She'll probably even tell you where she got the recipe. Now, if you ask her what she had for breakfast, she'll most likely have forgotten. But, that's another story.

Willie is so well known for her pies that around Thanksgiving she has orders for them. Our hairdresser is her biggest fan but I think Mike is a close second. If you think her hair looks pretty smart when you see her it's because she can bake a mean pie. No kidding.

So here is how Willie recites her recipe.

"This is a Betty Crocker recipe so don't say it's my recipe, okay? So, for two 9-inch pie crusts, you take 2/3 cups lard, a pinch of salt, and two cups flour. You cut the lard into the flour. You can use a food processor. I do sometimes, but usually I just do it by hand. Add in ¼ cup cold water. You're supposed to let it cool first but I just want to get it done, so I never do. (*No wonder we're good friends!*) Roll it out to fit your pan. Do you need more instructions than that?"

"Nope. That's good," I say, knowing darn well that when I try her recipe, it won't come out nearly the same. Willie just has the magic touch when it comes to baking.

7. Sick Day
February 3, 2017

Both Mike and I have been sick. Together, we spent more than a month fighting off what appears to be a combination of a cold and bronchitis. When you are sick, the whole world takes on a dark hue. You feel so lifeless and brittle that any little thing can upset your whole perspective on life and your life choices. Your friends want you to play but you can't. They ask you questions like, "Why are you sick?"

Because your immunity to life's silly questions are low, you try to justify why you, even *you,* the purported "pusher" of all things healthy could actually be sick. You come up with reasons and the answer is pretty simple. Well, because people get sick.

While I am going through it, I start to consider myself a sickly person. I can't help it. I start to ruminate on all of the times I got sick and I start to question my own sanity (well, health). But when it's finally all over, and I am back to my normal happy healthy self, I realize that what cured me from being sick was the rest I needed.

It is inevitable that after everything is said and done, I have looked back on my "sick days" as gifts from a higher source. They were the days that forced me to spend a little time writing a chapter or working on a puzzle in the daylight when you can really see the pieces. All the better if my best friend is sick at the same time. We can spend quality time together revisiting a puzzle that is getting a little worn but is still a challenge.

Today, it is the puzzle that looks just like our little cabin in a winter woods scene. Now that we know how to build a log cabin, putting together the cabin part of the puzzle was easier. We agreed that the hardest part is still the stack of firewood in the bottom left corner. But I discovered something this time that I think might be an important observation for puzzlers everywhere.

When you are trying to find a piece that fits in a spot or an area, you have to remind yourself that it is a painting, not a photograph. That means that when you are separating out, say, the colored pieces for snow, you have to remember that the artist might have chosen a deep purple color to depict the snow in an area. Your mind thinks, "Purple... snow is NOT purple..." but it actually is in this case.

It always amazes me how, when I can shift my perspective, something that has been right in front of me, a possible solution, perhaps (usually something so simple) just jumps out and becomes apparent. It was a puzzle piece that was sitting right next to the spot where it belonged the whole time but I could not see how it fit. The only way that I can *see* it is to stop and reset my perspective. Getting sick has proven to be one of the best ways to force this kind of slow down. (Who knows, maybe someday I will be able to forgo the sickness and get right to the slowdown.)

Since January 3rd, I have been a little swamped at work, trying to plan for five different levels of Spanish, deal with middle-schoolers, and take an online course that taxes my technical abilities. All of this started at the same time that I was scheduled to do my morning duty which entailed monitoring the cafeteria (mostly middle-schoolers) forty minutes a day before school starts. This duty seriously cut into my early morning planning time which had shifted into a schedule that sometimes only provided me an hour and forty minutes of plan time a week. None of my classes are study halls.

If you never taught, consider that with three minutes between classes, there is not a lot of time for a teacher to take a bathroom break with this kind of schedule. But I have no room to complain, all of my colleagues have it the same.

It is part of teaching in a small school where everybody is needed all day long to monitor students. It is just the way it is. We all do our best to teach our subjects enthusiastically and to plan interesting and exciting lessons that our students, parents, and administrators expect from us without much time built into the day to plan, let alone use the facilities.

To be honest, I was getting a little grumpy about my choice to go back to school. Today's students are reared with the idea that they are the consumers of public education and in our culture, we teach that the customer is always right. Kids know how to maximize that kind of empowerment and muck up the works of a well-meaning teacher very easily. The funny thing is that when a class gets out of control, the first question that comes to mind is always, "Well, what is that teacher doing?"

Since your immunities are so low, your first response is to answer that dumb question and justify how you, yes, even *you,* could have "allowed" your class to get out of control. The real answer is, "because they are kids and they are going to try and mess up the adults in their world as best they can. If they know that parents and administrators are going to blame the teacher for an out-of-control classroom, they are going to be like wolves on a kill. They head straight for the jugular. That's why."

So, how can a shift in perspective make this situation better? Well, a sick day can help. Most of us won't take a sick day unless we are truly sick. I had decided to go to my doctor and make sure I did not have pneumonia. As it turns out, it's just a post nasal drip and all of a sudden, I feel much better. This is just another example of how a shift in perspective can change things.

The other thing that happened with the forced rest is that I came up with a solution to the problem of dealing with my students. I have been feeling a certain hostility from *some of them* and the forced rest has made it clear to me that most of them are perfectly pleasant and kind. There are a few pieces to the puzzle that must be set aside and will fit in at the end. It is best not to focus on them too much at the moment because it will stymie my progress.

Part of my duties as a teacher include being a freshman class advisor. I have to attend their executive board meetings and watch while they all talk over each other, negate any new ideas, and carry the conflict with each other into their classes where it becomes high drama. I am treated with the same disrespect if I offer advice.

Like a lot of schools in our country, most of our students come from what we refer to as "broken homes"; many have "learning disabilities"; many of them are in foster care; some of them are homeless. When you add up all of the excuses for poor behavior, anything can be justified. The truth is, it often is.

My shift in perspective this time is not so much about how I am going to survive being back in school again as it is about what I am going to teach my students about survival. What came to me last night while my mind was finally rested, was the missing puzzle piece that was sitting there all along.

While it is clear that my students have a lot of baggage they have to deal with (some things I have never had to deal with; and some things I have had to deal with I hope to God, they never will have to deal with), they are best served to learn some people skills.

When I go back in on Monday, I am going to emphasize people skills in my daily dealings with each of them. I am going to demonstrate how a simple smile is the start to a good day. I am going to teach them how to "fake it 'till you make it" and how much the little things matter. I am going to talk to my freshmen about saying less and listening more. I am going to teach them about edifying others.

I know that it sounds idealistic but I think that if I am attentive, I can do it. I can make it a point to try and teach one personal skill a day to some student who needs it and demonstrate one of the skills to all.

"Perspective means that if you look at all of your students as little devils, then it is easy to assume you are in Hell. You just have to look at it differently," Mike reminds me.

He follows this statement with, "The lighthouse doesn't do anything to try and calm the seas. It just points the way." I hold this little talisman close to my heart as I return to work. His analogy is a beacon of truth for my storm-weary spirit.

Yes, being sick has given me the chance to reset my attitude. I am back in school to teach students much-needed skills. I am here to help them also see that if they view all of their teachers as mean demons, they will think they are in Hell too. And the truth is, it is all too easy to become a mean demon when a couple of little devils try to push you into out-devilling them, especially when your immunities are low.

THIEVES OIL

Thieves Oil is a special mixture of essential oils that not only smells warm and refreshing but has potent antibacterial and antiviral properties. The legend of Thieves Oil is that five thieves used it to protect themselves from the Plague during the Medieval Period. They apparently learned to blend these oils and place the blend in a cone-shaped mask so they could enter the Plague victims' homes and steal their belongings.

Fast forward seven centuries and picture microbiologists in a lab testing bleach and other chemicals on their efficacy in killing germs on contact. The line-up included commercial cleaners, alcohol wipes, pine cleaners, and Thieves Oil. Bleach took first place with Thieves Oil coming in second. I don't know about you but I'm not putting bleach anywhere near my skin, clothes, or anything but countertops and sinks.

I would, however, put Thieves Oil on my hands, around the base of my neck, under my nose, or anywhere else I could use a little barrier against germs and bugs. Some people put it on the soles of their feet before going to bed.

You can buy Thieves Oil already mixed and sold commercially. It is a bit pricey and usually comes in half-ounce bottles. But, you can also mix your own. The initial investment in essential oils can be more than buying the oil already mixed so you'll have to make that judgement call.

So here's the recipe for a one-ounce bottle. Put your oil mixtures in small colored bottles so that sunlight does not change them. I use grapeseed oil as the base oil. It is light, odorless, and you can usually find it in big box stores. It is also recommended to use a few drops of vitamin E oil to preserve your essential oil mixtures.

20 drops clove essential oil
10 drops cinnamon essential oil
18 drops lemon essential oil
8 drops eucalyptus essential oil
5 drops rosemary essential oil

As you probably can tell by the ingredients, it has a complex yet pleasingly warm and bright fragrance that you can keep on hand during cold season. (Quite literally on hand(s), feet, and neck.) If it weren't so creepy looking, you could place it in a surgical mask at work when everyone starts sneezing into the air vents. Believe me, I have thought about it.

8. The Grid
March 19, 2017

We are float-charging today. It is a sunny day and we are generating lots of power that we are storing in our twelve 6 volt batteries that we have boxed up in the basement. It is warm enough now that the snow has melted off of the panels so we are fully charging.

Going solar has been trickle-charging in my mind since I was in my twenties. I have been reading whatever came my way about people who were living off-grid. I read about how some people were making adobe-styled homes out of old tires and sand-filled rice bags in the deserts of Nevada. I loved to hear what people were coming up with so that they could unleash from the ordinary.

If you could make something beautiful and useful out of something that is a spot on human existence like old tires, why not? These things fascinated me. I owned the first of the solar-powered radios and flashlights, thinking solar-powered stoves and ovens would be perfect for places like

Haiti where cutting down trees for firewood has decimated the forests and jungles.

For a while, though, it seemed as though the innovations in technology were slowing down. It appeared that there would be only solar radios and keychain flashlights in my off-grid living. Capturing the sun's power could not create enough heat to cook a meal. The Haitians would have to wait.

Today, however, there are so many companies creating solar power panels and technology that the pieces are beginning to fit together more easily. Prices for panels and technology are becoming more reasonable and the panels are more efficient. Chances are that in the next ten years, solar will become a good solution to human needs like cooking and lighting.

What could be simpler than amplifying the sun's heat to create the power we need? What has taken so long to harness that incredible power? The answer is that it's not really as simple as all that. For one thing, we think of solar power as so "green" (a heavy word for a little middle-road color!). It is just sun and no byproduct, right? Yeah, no.

For one thing, you need batteries. We use wet-cell batteries that create no real hazardous waste because they will be 100% recycled at the end of eight years. We use an equalizer that shakes the scale off the plates. It helps them last a little longer. Once a month, Mike makes sure they have their distilled water topped off.

Then there is the converter. That is where the real technology is. The charge controller gathers the electricity from the panel and uses that energy to charge the batteries. The inverter takes the DC (direct current - a straight line) from the batteries and turns it into AC (alternating current – a wave-type current) which travels farther. It can travel a long distance without drop-off.

Edison, who thought AC was too dangerous, was a proponent of DC but that shorter-distance direct current required the that he propose that every street and every block would have its own power plant. Tesla and Westinghouse promoted AC current and demonstrated that it was safe and superior at the Chicago World Fair.

The shorter DC (direct current) is what your battery chargers use but they have to invert the current back from AC that comes out of your plug. That is why chargers always have an awkward inverter boxes attached to their cables or at the outlet.

With solar power, you might have 80 volts of AC coming out of the panels but it would blow up the system so the charge controller takes the power and leads it to the batteries without overcharging them, much like the little box on your laptop battery chargers, it converts the energy to DC. The batteries are connected to a DC converter which is hooked up to the solar panels and leads to the batteries to transform the absorption of sunlight into useable storable.

A solar inverter changes the stored energy back into AC so that it can leave the electrical outlets at a normal rate to power household appliances and lights. The ironic thing is that when you plug in your phone or laptop to charge, it has to convert that AC power back to DC to become stored power in your phone battery or laptop battery. Funny.

It all sounds ideal for those of us who would like to see less drilling, pumping, and spilling of petroleum products. But the reality is a little more complex than all that. It is important that we don't take a broad brush and paint the world in one tone of green when it comes to managing the human impact on the world and each other. We are going to leave a mark. Ants do it. Porcupines do it. The predators do it. And the ones they eat do it. The only difference is that we are self-conscious. We know that we leave a mark and we feel that it is our responsibility to be in harmony with the rest of nature. Perhaps that is why the writers of human history as we know it, claimed that we were to tend to the gardens and the beasts.

The reality is, there is an "ungreen" side of solar that still must be contended with. For one thing, all of the materials that go into solar panels must be manufactured like anything else. The plastic around the wires, the wires themselves, the glass, the lead and acid for the batteries are all products of drilling and mining.

The real problem is a chemical called NF-3 Nitrogen Trifloride that is used in the production of the panels. NF3 is 17,000 times more potent than CO2 as a greenhouse gas.

But, even with this fact, I still believe small solar power generators is the way to go. I think it would be good to see more houses off grid. Other than the need for a decent road, it makes house placement more in alignment with nature and its beauty. If your house is not tethered to the grid, you can put it where you want it, regardless of main roads and electrical hook-ups. Too often people are obliged to put their houses close to the road because of the grid. There are other considerations too. Up here, it is also about the amount of snow you have to remove to get in and out but that can be reckoned with too.

Living off-grid, we are simply not aware when there is a power outage because we are not connected. That, and the fact that our system is paid for and any additional costs are scheduled and in the budget (batteries) so there are no unexpected price hikes or random spikes in usage that need to be discussed with an unwilling representative from the electric company. Any future expenses will probably be lower than budgeted since the technology gets better and less expensive every year. One of the pluses of not having power is that you never lose it.

Mike and I were having dinner in our local restaurant recently and could not help but overhear a group of ladies at a table next to us comparing their electric bills.

Numbers such as 179 and 280 were thrown around the table as the ladies were comparing their electric bills. Their friendly competition and laughing attitudes belied the fact that this certainly is the reality of most Americans, if not people around the world. Mike and I just gave each other the look.

When other tables got involved in the conversation, Mike had to chime in, "We live off-grid. We have no electric bill."

People have become slaves to these huge energy conglomerates. We obviously have choices. We could use less. We could invest in an expensive solar set-up to sell electricity back to the company but that requires too much investment on our part. It also requires that we still be hooked to the grid, the electric company sets its own buy-back prices, and the company can change its policies on buy-backs whenever it suits them. You could argue that if that begins to happen, then you can just disconnect the electric company's wires to your home and reconnect a home-based inverter and charge controller for energy independence at that point. It is even interesting that some states like Florida have used legislation to make it more difficult to live off-grid.

There are so many good reasons to disconnect. The quiet alone is worth it. When you can position your house back from the road, life takes on a certain tranquility that the noise of human activity forces out. Obviously, the further from the epicenter of activity you get, the easier it is to find that tranquility. Add to that the choices that must be made. For instance, is that large plasma TV really worth the energy draw? How about the microwave? You get the drift. All of those things that can make your life more comfortable may be causing an opposite effect in the long run.

Having a partner who was willing to try making off-grid living work has been pretty amazing. But, I am willing to bet that most Americans (and others around the world) have had a similar vision. It is a small step, to cut the wires and go solo.

All it takes is some research, some saving up in advance, and the faith that things will be just fine without that bill in the mail. The good news is that it is getting more and more manageable all of the time. And, the more of us who do it, the more accessible the dream gets.

SOLAR AND WIND

For one reason or another, there are a lot of people who live off-grid in Maine. We have friends from all walks of life, with all kinds of viewpoints and ideologies who live off-grid.

Our friends Lyn and Kent, built their house on 100 acres across the river from us and considered that they just needed a house that would keep them warm in the winter since they spend most of their time outside. The placement of their house was more than a mile from the nearest electric pole. When we met them, they used a battery system with a generator that they kept going almost consistently, especially at night when Kent used his CPAC to sleep. It also powered a very interesting geothermal heating system that Kent improvised to keep their basement warm since that is where he had his workshop.

In order to power all of the things they needed, they invested in a larger solar array than the one we had at the time. The payoff has been tremendous, however, since they no longer have to keep the generator going.

We have another set of friends, Karla and Roy, who began their off-grid experience with four young children back in the early 1980's when solar powered homes were just making their debut. As a result, they claim, they spent a lot of money on their first systems. Roy is the classic inventor type and knows way more than anyone I have ever met about off-grid technology. Raising a family increases some energy needs (in more ways than one). That is why they included a wind turbine that they used for many years that made up the difference in the solar-generated power as a result of the shorter winter days.

Eventually, Roy explained, he dismantled the wind turbine because it was too much maintenance and their improved solar made up the difference they were originally missing in the shorter winter days. Maintenance on solar panels means raking them off after a heavy snow.

Maintenance on a wind turbine means making sure you don't run it when too much ice collects on the blades, and since it is an engine on a 40-100 foot tower that is exposed to minimum and sustained 5 mph winds and vibrates accordingly, there will be bolts and parts that must be replaced continuously.

When considering using wind power, make sure you investigate thoroughly and do not believe the sales pitches. It is commonly known in the field that wind power distributors exaggerate the output and will not disclose how important it is that your site has sufficient wind and no turbulence. If you are grid-tied and are looking into wind power, it is also advised that you not just settle on the list of distributors and manufacturers that the electric company provides. That is a self-generated list, kind of like the yellow pages. Companies pay to be on the list. Another thing to watch out for is that if you try to go with the most economical product out there, many times their turbines are not tested and can break down within minutes of installation.

There is so much to learn when it comes to off-grid living. Unless you are an intrepid inventor and just want to see things for yourself, creating your own DIY turbines might not give you the return that you are looking for. There is the vertical vs. horizontal (egg-beater vs. fan-type) to consider. But that is too much information to include here.

I'm not saying that it isn't worth trying it. I'm just saying spend a lot of time researching it before you dish out any dough. Eventually small wind turbines might catch up to the efficiency of solar but it has not happened yet. Our friend, Lee, who has been installing alternative energy systems for over thirty years calls them nice lawn ornaments.

Another thing to think about is passive solar. Our friends Lyn and Kent have a south-facing wall that is almost completely windows. That alone cuts down on the amount of wood they need to heat their house. This results in less energy and time in the fall when they stack wood. We enlisted the passive solar technique when we closed in our front deck and added windows to the south side of the house. The room also acts like an insulating buffer against the cold.

When considering solar and wind, it is best to think about the orientation of your home since that will determine your most efficient use of your life's energy.

Note: As a simple reference: Solar power per watt is much less expensive now. Twenty years ago, a $700 panel would generate 25 watts. Today, the same sized panel costs $180 and generates 320 watts. Every year, all of the components of a solar system get more efficient and less expensive.

9. Fiddleheads
May 12, 2017

It is Friday. All of my foraging friends have been out *fiddleheading* because the weather has finally broken in. They are delicately and quietly making their way to their spots, trying not to step on fern shoots as they go. I, on the other hand, just experienced the onslaught of a wild pack of eighth grade boys and girls who are supposed to be learning Spanish.

I know that I will have plenty of time to forage in July – just when the berries pop. I am not as interested in pickling or freezing fiddleheads. I just want to eat them fresh, that's all. So, I will have to get out there on a weekend when I can and pick some for dinner.

I will have to go out with Willie, though. We will need to talk about stuff on the way out there. We will have to stop and notice some new mushroom on a tree or scope out the bald eagle's nest. We will have to check the birches for chaga. We will have to notice whether the trout lilies are robust this year, stop and munch on a few, and gather them for our salads. We will muse over how much skunk cabbage moved in. We will have to make sure to keep an eye out for ramps since they like the same places as fiddlers. It's always more than about filling the bucket when Willie and I go out.

When I stop to think about it, the problem with those eighth grade boys and girls is that they truly are wild. I wish I could just take them outside on this perfect sunny day, let them get muddy and a little cold. I wish I could let them learn a few things about the power of calm. I wish I could take them out with Willie to learn something meaningful.

Our youth is our spring and right now the sap is rising and their feeder limbs are growing faster than their trunks. The problem with many of our youth is that they are lacking a good, solid root system that schools just cannot provide. The only way to learn the kind of calm Willie could teach them is to be out one-on-one with someone of that generation and learn the names of the wildflowers and the trees from someone who learned it that way from a grandparent. Understanding the woods and fields is a true folk art. It must be done through an oral tradition with hands-on learning. Around here, they call that being *woodswise.*

Many of my friends are involved with outdoor schooling. I believe that we need to make more of our schooling outdoors. If students could feel the cold wind needle its way through the holes in their gear, they might be more interested in learning how to make a fire. They might be happier to be sitting in a nice warm classroom after getting wet and cold. Or maybe they would still rather be outside feeling the wind.

What my friends like Claudia, Deneen, and Dena do is they teach children how to respect nature and each other through adventures where they have to do some creative problem-solving and work together. They learn how to forage for their nighttime teas, how to find water sources and how to purify the water once they find it. They teach how to forage and hunt and what to do with the hide once you catch your prey. They run programs all year long for adults and children.

With so much of this going on in Maine and so many of our youth already involved in hunting and many of these skills, why not make this an integral part of our teaching day. As it turns out, some schools in Maine are doing just that. They are incorporating more and more outdoor education into their school day.

I am not sure what it would look like exactly, and I know it would take a village of people to make it work, but I think it could be a good answer to many of our little school's problems.

I am sure the reason why my eighth graders are so squirrelly is because it is the best day we have had this month and, like me, they have been waiting for it since Ray Bradbury wrote *All Summer in a Day*. Nevertheless, they are stuck in a classroom being told they must sit still and copy notes when all they want to do is run. I get it. I feel the exact same way.

The best I can do right now is move my classroom outside and let my students pick the dandelions on the school grounds since our maintenance guy, Donnie, assured me that they do not spray any weed-killer on the lawn. We will take them back into class and make fritters out of them.

We might do the same with the Japanese knotweed. It is not traditional Spanish food but I feel pretty confident that if my Costa Rican grandmother were here, she would invent a pretty good recipe for a Japanese knotweed green salsa. I might have to try it.

My time with Willie is precious and I know it. We share not just our love for nature and the quiet, but we share our lives. Setting out to pick fiddleheads is just the incentive to be outside for an extended period of time, to get muddy and a little uncomfortable.

Willie is a walking guidebook. When you go out to pick fiddlers, you'll learn that the ferns with the fuzzy coatings will give you diarrhea, and the other ones, called cinnamon ferns are no good either but their spores give off a little brown powder that looks like cinnamon.

Willie does pickle her fiddlers so she gathers quite a bit of them. The problem is that they are wrapped in a brown paper bag coating that is wound into the tight spiral of their heads and it takes a bit of work to get rid of it. That's why a friend of hers invented a cylindrical cage made from chicken wire that is attached to a gear and a handle so she just puts her fiddlers on a spin cycle and tumbles the little paper bags right out of them. What you have left is a good bucketful of glossy, dark green spirals that are crisp and tasty.

The problem with fiddlers is that people sometimes get a little too voracious in their appetite for the money they can make on these exotic foods. Or they get carried away on stocking up on "free food." I have been guilty of that on occasion. I still have a packet of frozen fiddleheads in my freezer from last year.

It makes harvesting wild foods a dangerous balancing act because once a food or product becomes the one everyone is talking about, it becomes scarce. Too many people harvesting unethically can be devastating. That's why a forager never tells where she goes unless it is to a good friend who can keep it close to her chest. Even so, that friend may end up sharing with another close friend and there you have it. Foraging friendships are different. They can only exist between people who can keep secrets.

To be honest, I'm keeping Willie and her "spot" close to my chest. I don't mind sharing dandelions, autumn olives, and Japanese knotweeds and any other of the "weeds" that humans consider annoying with my eighth graders. Somehow, picturing twenty-five pairs of rubber boots trampling over the delicate little fiddlers in any one of our "spots" is enough to make me cringe. Taking it in little bits is how things are done right. Given time and some planning, maybe we can find a way to open the doors of the school, let boys and girls be a little wild, and teach them how to protect what is delicate and quiet.

RAMP BUTTER

Fiddleheads are a delicious wild food and they are a lot of fun to harvest but my favorite green wild food is ramps, a type of leek. The fresh vibrancy of these low-growing emerald beauties is out-of-this world delicious when you could really use a splash of green in the middle of winter.

I love basil and always try to set up as much pesto as possible in the summer when the basil bolts but basil loses its green vibrancy as soon as it is processed. The same happens with parsley, sage, and other herbs like rosemary and thyme. (I'm feeling a Simon and Garfunkle song coming on.)

Ramps maintain their green color when you use them to make a pesto. They also have a tangy flavor that can clear your sinuses like onions and garlics sometimes do, but it is not overpowering.

Ramps grow in early spring when the trees have no leaves. They like sunlight that is filtered through the bare branches and the loamy soil that collects under deciduous trees. Ramps (also called wild leeks) are presently considered endangered, probably due to over harvesting. What my friends and I do is transplant small patches in similar spots to propagate the species. We also harvest ethically by only taking one of the two leaves that stem out of the thin reddish-purple "bulb." When harvesters dig up the entire plant, it is unsustainable.

Ramp pesto is wonderful but our favorite treat is ramp butter. Butter, we have discovered, is an excellent way to preserve the flavor and vibrancy of a lot of fresh herbs. Sage butter is a culinary miracle that is perfect for potatoes, pasta, breads, and is a decadent accent on meats such as chicken and steak. Ramp butter is even better.

To make your herb butters, you take a piece of parchment paper that is at least 10" long and soften a pound of butter so that it can be easily molded but is not runny. Pulse at least a cup of fresh herbs and a little salt in your blender or food processor until it is chopped finely. Add half of the butter and pulse again until you get a paste. Spoon it out onto one-third of the parchment paper. Add the two butter sticks by slicing them lengthwise.

Use the parchment paper to create a long log by rolling the butter filling in the parchment paper. Roll it quite a bit to integrate the plain butter into the herb butter and to create an even tube shape about an inch and a half in diameter.

Place in the freezer to harden before cutting. After cutting into rounds, store the little gems in your freezer in a plastic bag to use as an accent flavor any time you would like to add a little zing to your thing.

10. Guru
June 17, 2017

Yesterday was the last day of school and I made a trip to the local grocery store. I have begun to take it for granted that I am going to run into someone I know when I am in town. I don't realize how much that happens until I visit my parents in South Florida and I see how they might not even know the cashier at their grocery store. I know all of the workers at the local stores. Some of them are my students. But mostly, even if it is their first day on the job, they all wear name tags. It's only fair to introduce myself too. A little conversation while they scan and you swipe your card or dig for change makes the world a better place.

Yesterday was a banner day for running into people I know. Since it was Friday, there was no reason to rush any of my encounters. First, there was Johnny, the man who did the excavation for our foundation and did so much more than that for us. His granddaughter won the local prize for a poem she wrote called, "The Best Grampy Ever" and because of social media, I had read the poem and could comment on the cuteness of it. In reasonable fashion, he told me more about his grandchildren and I listened with all of the appropriate and genuine smiles and chuckles.

I had been interviewed (again this year) for the Black Fly Festival and it must have been a slow news week because apparently that reel of me was broadcast repeatedly on Channel 5 news. Since I don't have a TV, I only saw it once on social media. Johnny told me that the little kids who followed me on the reel were his grandchildren. That fact still gives me a chuckle. They were all excited about the parade because they got candy.

That fact may not seem all that important but Johnny's grandson said he thought it was good because some kids don't get candy and it was a chance for them all to get something. Revisiting this comment made me ponder. The Black Fly Festival is a chance for us all to participate in ways that are accessible. For me, it is a chance to introduce my newest book, put out some beeswax candles and salves to sell, and promote my yoga class. Willie, who has been learning how to throw pots too, shared my tent and was able to sell some of her pottery. We made a little money and provided a little color to the town. There was live music, the parade, and vendors from in town and out who all had something (usually handmade) to sell. It is a good thing.

So, after getting swiped by the grocery store door a couple of times, Johnny and I decided it was time to end our conversation and go about our ways. He was going out. I was going in.

Seeing Ellen enter the store made the transition a little easier. I followed her in, noticing that she looked a little stiff. Now, it is my habit to notice these things. Ellen was one of the first people to come to my yoga class when we started about four or five years ago. But her schedule has made it more difficult to get to class. I was able to tell her about my summer hours and it made her happy to know that she will be able to attend.

I don't remember what else we talked about but I know we both parted laughing. We both had some business to do in the produce section. Organic lettuce or not...? What's the price on those Brussels now? You know, important stuff like that.

That's when I saw my accountant, Brenda, and her husband, Don, in a quandary over a package of tofu. They were huddled over the plastic container like it was a science experiment and seemed to be disagreeing over the results.

"Hey, what's up guys?!" That was my way of butting in.

"We are trying to lose weight and eat healthier," Brenda answered.

"Well, I HAVE lost weight," Don said.

"Well, I have too," she said.

"Yes, you both look great!" I responded. It was true.

"Well, I read that you shouldn't eat a lot of tofu," she added. "What do you think?"

I said that I had also heard that the latest research on soy products seem to indicate not to eat it but that the Japanese have been eating it for eons and seem to be okay so far. "Besides, all of this research comes from the same people who say eggs are bad for you... eggs are good for you...butter is bad... butter is good..."

"Well, should we eat it or not? Aren't you the guru on all of this stuff?" Don laughed and mimicked the international sign language gesture of meditating by making the okay sign with both hands and closing his eyes.

"Yeah, I put the goo in roo," I said as I thought about what I had come to the grocery store to get. It certainly was not tofu!

I left as he was reading the fine print on the back of the package out loud.

So, I headed off to the chip isle. Listen, it was the last day of school and I was certainly not going to try and make Mike eat tofu for dinner. Besides, he claims it is his spirit animal and he is forbidden to eat it.

And then I grabbed a six pack of Moosehead beer because it is cheap.

That's when I got in line behind Ellen at the register. In a small town you can't pretend you didn't see someone, even if you would like to. So, Ellen, who had stocked up at the deli says, "Wow, I wouldn't have expected to see you with chips."

"Oh, yeah, anyone who knows me knows what a chip junkie I am." I am not proud of this fact but I am not ashamed either. It might be what does me in eventually. I'm sure when I die, someone is going to say, *It was probably that chip habit she had... calcified her liver, I'd say..."* But by then, I won't have any care for my liver. I'm sure it will be lightly salted. Today, I just want to relax with a bag of chips and some beer. Let the chips fall where they may.

"I am always so embarrassed to buy processed American cheese but my husband loves it," Ellen confessed. I don't understand it since he's from England and they have the best cheeses there. But, I can't convince him. Who knows what is in that stuff."

I'm thinking, yeah, I can't convince Mike to eat tofu. In a lot of ways, the male partner in the relationship tends to indicate what is eaten in the house. It is just an observation and I'm sure I am wrong...but we influence each other. Besides, I think it has more to do with our efforts to make the other person happy. Food choices are just as much about being happy as anything else.

For Mike and me, it makes us happy to buy our milk straight from our farmer. If we pick the milk up together, we generally stop along the road to drink the cream right off the top. If we happen to run into Wendy busily haying the goats or rounding up the chickens for the night, we stop and say hi to her. Happy farmer, happy cows, happy customer. It's the ultimate food chain.

For me, foraging is the same thing. It gives me a chance to coordinate schedules with friends and Mother Nature to get outside and connect to something greater than our daily lives. It is about opening up that little green packet of frozen ramp butter in the middle of February to spice up my roasted Brussel sprouts. That is happiness too.

Seeing Brenda and Don huddled over the little plastic box of tofu is a happy moment. It was a celebration of sorts. A wedding of minds towards a common goal. Here we are, folks, loving each other so much that we want to live as long and healthy a life together as we can. We want to have the energy to make it to church on Sunday after a full week of a stressful commute to a job that may not be as fulfilling as we would like just so we can enjoy simple comforts together.

I laugh at the word choice. *Guru.* I might not know a lot of questions but I certainly don't know any of the answers.

As is my nature, I ponder the word. And, as with any word, our thoughts about it give it the meaning. It does mean teacher, I think to myself. It means life, love, the ability to laugh in the face of the World's decided lack of humor. It means helping others to find the light in their darkest corners. It means being there. Being silent. Having no answers. Leading by following behind so the stragglers know there is always someone a little slower than they are.

It means being in the world but not of it. It means being able to see the beauty in a package of tofu, in a slice of cheese, in the achiness, the suffering, the swearing of adolescents who know not what they do. It means wearing a smile every day and being genuine in that smile. It means living your practice. All that and a bag of chips.

Add a little discount beer and I'll take it.

MAKING HARD CIDER

Making your own hard cider is one of those things that, once you have the right tools, is pretty easy. All you have to do is mash up your apples (to be honest, the wild ones and crabapples are best and using apples that are all beaten up and will go unused is satisfying). Our friends use a wood chipper that they save just for apples and then they use a cider press to squeeze out all of the juice.

We do not own that kind of equipment so we get together with our friends who do and bring enough wild apples to share with the group of folks who gather to do their apple pressing. This is the hardest part, if you can call getting together with friends and talking apples and sharing last year's ciders and meads a hard thing.

When you get home with your five gallon bucket of apple juice, you add a little yeast. The health food stores often have a section on fermenting and will have a few different types of yeast that are good for cider. The truth is that cider has its own yeast so this part is unnecessary but does help if you would like to control how your cider comes out.

It is helpful to have a big glass container with a narrow neck. The proper term for that container is a *carboy*. The only other thing you need to make your own hard cider is a type of valve that allows air to escape but not to enter. That is called an *airlock* and works simply by creating a space where the air can bubble out through a small amount of water which forms a seal so that air can't enter.

We keep our carboy upstairs in the winter where it is warmest in the house. After about a month or so, you'll notice that the apple sediments (pulp) have collected in the bottom so you use a syphon hose to remove the clear liquid on top and then discard the pulpy sediment. It is always good to clean the carboy when you do this. This is called *racking your cider*. Let it sit for another month or so and then repeat the racking. Do this again for some really great cider. By the time the weather begins to turn and you anticipate the day when you could really use a nice cold one, your cider is ready to bottle up. We add a ¼ teaspoon of brown sugar to each bottle so that it ferments just enough to fizz but not enough to pop the top in your basement. So good! It is worth trying it with other fruits if you aren't in apple country.

10. Neutrality
June 20, 2017

Very few things are as controversial as neutrality but I happen to like it. For one thing, you have to trust that there is a bigger plan in place in order to maintain neutrality. I am fond of little quips (sorry Emerson, I can't help quoting someone today!). One of my favorites is, "Things are neither good nor bad, 'tis thinking that makes them so." That reportedly was Shakespeare. I believe it because I think the old bard was definitely a fan of how powerful the human brain is.

One time before yoga class, my students and I were talking about in-laws and how to avoid conflict. That's when Mary Ellen said that her mother used to always tell her to "just wear beige and keep your mouth closed." To me, that was the ultimate in good advice about how to preserve neutrality. The only difference is that I wear grey because beige does not look good on me.

We are so easily led into thinking and believing the most ridiculous things. It is never completely evident until years or even decades later when we look back and question why we or anyone ever thought certain things. I guess that's why I got rid of our TV more than twelve years ago. I saw how it was twerking the minds of my family in ways that were not good for them. It is an insidious companion for many of us that does a number on our ability to remain balanced.

We are not going to be able to escape the pulls on minds, emotions, and wallets in this world of modern lifestyle. It would be ridiculous to think we could ever be immune. If you are tempted to think there is a place on earth that is completely immune from pulls on the psyche, consider that pulls also may come from traditional values or tribal beliefs. I would wager that no one of us on this planet is completely immune from influences that pull us off balance.

So, what is a person to do? How can we live in the world and still maintain some sort of stability? Is it possible? These are the questions I ask after spending the last school year struggling with balance and repairing my emotional shields from the chinks caused by that kind of work. It is important to try and never take anything personally when the sharp arrows of judgement penetrate the shield and you come home with both a wound and an expensive maintenance plan on your armor.

Without going into too much personal detail, let's just say that my armor was battered a bit this year and I am taking the time I need to patch up the dents and polish up the surface. My summer maintenance plan includes taking time for a little jog through the woods with Hermes. We are scoping out if any mushrooms have sprouted and seeing where the blackberry brambles are blossoming. A comprehensive maintenance plan includes whether the little nettle patch I planted has rooted, and what kind of wildlife activity there has been.

It has been raining heavily so the bugs are scurrying to the surface to avoid their flooded homes and the worms are growing fat with the moisture. It is a choice time to let our chickens out to forage on the protein feast and keep the critters at bay.

Ticks have been a huge problem this year with all of the moisture. I have already found two on me. I suffered quite a bit from Lyme disease about ten years ago so I am a bit cautious when it comes to ticks but I refuse to let fear create a hole in my armor. The key to the word *disease* is the way that the deficit of ease works on us.

It creates a gaping hole in our armor and then the critters come in. They can't help but be attracted to the light that shines through the perforated mettle. It does not surprise me that both ticks settled in right around my heart center – the first one on my lower left shoulder and the second one on the left side of my chest. Little buggers. I cannot help but consider that tics are of the arachnid family – tiny little spiders.

But, I am not worried. I recognize the patterns that lead to the chinks in my armor and am working on changing those patterns. Armor is good but you have to be a warrior to be able to wear it. That means fearlessness and neutrality. Everyone knows that if you let the fight get into you, you have already lost the battle. You cannot win a battle if you go in with fear. It will send you reeling because you are off balance.

Thoughts and words help; time to repair and feel the presence of the silence will help. Sitting by the river helps.

It is a deep reminder that no matter what happens, life still goes on.   The river has its seasons and so will we all. Some late August days the river might be so low that the bedrock is exposed and one can walk directly across from shore to shore. By the time fall sets in, the river has reached impossible lows and seems as though all is lost. But, it only takes a few days of heavy rain to bring it back up to its normal range.

Because of that, and the fact that the river washes everything away, I see the river as the ultimate place to restore my neutrality. Combine yoga with the meditative flow of the river and you have a good recipe for shield mending at its finest.

The river doesn't care much what opinions you hold. The river just is. It is greater than any of us. It will be here long after any of us are gone and supports life that we are not even aware of. The river smooths out the edges of our shields so that they can glow with a luster that only time and a balanced spirit can create.

Any job can be rough on a person's shield. Teaching is just different because, as teacher, we must judge how to best maintain discipline in our classrooms and sometimes that requires calling a student out. The "calling out" energy very often is heightened and becomes a weapon that a student (and sometimes more) then uses to sling back at the teacher. It is an age-old problem. It just used to be that if a student was in trouble at school, it was not always assumed that it was a failing on the teacher's part.

Some days I just need to wear my armor of grey. It keeps me balanced and grounded so that I can be prepared for the counter-sling. Come to think of it, I have a lot of grey in my wardrobe.

Some people do not like it when you answer a controversial question with a neutral answer like, "I'm not sure." But most days, it is probably the most honest answer you can give. It is also a nice way to say, "Hey, I know you might be looking for a bit of provocation but I'm not engaging in that activity at the moment."

We all have a right to be neutral about things. It is the strongest stance to have. If we are honest, we will be able to admit that we don't have access to all of the information anyway and that sometimes a negative opinion can ruin something very positive. This is true of most debated issues today. Being neutral does not mean that you do not care. It means that you do not care to make a provocative issue a divisive one. I care more about my relationships than I do about appearing right on any issue. That is why sometimes I need to just wear grey and keep my mouth closed.

DEHYDRATED GREENS

One of the best things about summer, especially early summer is all of the leafy greens you can get. Our local farmer and his wife have a great farm stand that is always open. They use the honor system. If you aren't familiar with that system, it means that your farmer puts out a little metal box and you open it to put your money in it. You can also make change the same way. They don't ask you to write down what you bought. They know.

Mike and I love Swiss chard. We consider it part of our summer rites or is that summer…right…as in time to set things right. We figure that after a winter of heavy foods and sugary indulgences, our early summer greens help to neutralize our systems. Green, after all, along with yellow, is the middle color of the rainbow. It is the color of the heart center and it helps to balance things.

The problem is that sometimes we end up with a lot more of those leafy greens than we could possibly eat and neither of us likes to waste food if we can help it. So, we dehydrate our greens. It is amazing how much of the texture and nutrients dehydrating preserves.

The best greens for dehydrating are beet greens, kale, spinach, and chards. If you throw in a few of your wild greens, you have a superfood that you can add to any soup in the winter. Dried greens just pop right back up when you scoop up a handful and throw them into the pot once the soup is almost fully cooked.

12. Good Reads
July 6, 2017

"I think I need a good book that just pulls me in and sets me straight again. I miss Harold and wish I could go on his pilgrimage with him again." These are the kinds of conversations I can have with Mike. He remembers who Harold is (a character from a book we both read) and knows how hard it is for me to just be normal and enjoy a minute of peace sometimes. I was in that weird frame of mind that I can get into - that feeling of being rudderless. It's not that I have nothing to do. It's that I have put off doing the things I want to do for so long that I forgot how to get started doing them again.

Something about summer vacation after a year of school makes me, well, pardon the indulgence, a little off. I'm not sure exactly what happens, but I am sure that shifting from being so incredibly busy and adrenaline-driven to having no imminent pressure is disconcerting. I am derailed. I know that sounds a lot like whining to the rest of the world that gets two weeks of vacation, if lucky. Let's face it…it is whining!

And that makes it all worse. I have no right to be so melancholic about vacation time. I've just got so much of it. And Mike doesn't really enjoy my complaint as he heads off to work at 6 am every morning. But, anyway, that's how I ended up in the library, the sanctuary of all that is reasonable, on track, meaningful, and clear about life.

I had volunteered for the summer reading program and had gathered around me a little group of boys ranging from Joe, a twelve-year-old genius who loves science and knows his weight in guano about birds to Waylon, a three-year-old who lives up to his name quite properly and couldn't make it through the first two pages of *Curious George Goes to the Library*. I thought Waylon did an amazing job of doing live illustrations of little George in the library, kicking it up and causing havoc. I have to say, the workout he gives his mother is stellar and should be marketed. I was a little sad when he took off up the stairs and couldn't be convinced to join us again.

Other than the Curious George book, I asked the boys to pick out books they would like. We never did get to Waylon's books about motorcycles, which is unfortunate because I know nothing about them. Joe's little brother, Jake, picked out a bird book because he liked the colors. We were able to get through that whole book because of Joe. I couldn't help but wonder why our group was just boys but I was glad. I found a book about the innovative exploits of Leonardo da Vinci which seemed appropriate since our summer reading theme was "builders".

Since the book had a lot of text, and I knew I was losing my crowd, I improvised a little on the pictures from Leonardo's journals. I might have let slip that he used to sneak out in the middle of the night to cut open cadavers to see how the body works so he could draw and paint people better. And then there was Jesus having supper with a group of his friends before well, an unfortunate event happened and you can ask your grandma about that later.

Our librarian, Rochelle had given the kids little blow-up hammers that I'm sure the boys would use for deconstructive purposes later. Maybe the little book of poems titled, *I'm Allergic to School* gave them some ideas about how the hammers could be used in the back seat of grandma's car later. But hey, that was going way beyond my responsibility as the summer read-aloud volunteer. Whatever new ideas they get from reading is not my fault.

Having done my civic duty of stirring up the wild imaginations of rogue adventurers, I went upstairs to check out some books. Rochelle renewed the book Mike had next to his bed that I forgot to return for him. She's really kind like that. I saw a cool book about Red Cloud. It was very thick, about history, and the back of the book started with, "The word epic is highly overused…" I knew that would be great for Mike. It's exactly the kind of thing he would say about a book.

"I need something to keep my mind off of the fact that I have nothing to keep my mind on." I said to Kathy. I could hear the sigh. I know I am the hardest person to find a book for because I don't, well… I'm not your typical reader. I'm not what anyone would even call *a reader*.

But Kathy is, by far, the best librarian I have ever encountered when it comes to finding books for people. She has a certain ESP, extra-sensitive people-skill, when it comes to reading a person's reading.

Mike loves Kathy in a certain intimate way that only a good librarian can be loved. She knows exactly what to give him when he stops by for a book. It is always two books that are about completely different subjects because he might not be in the right mood for one but the other might be just right. "She nails it every time." The other thing he likes is that she will always ask what he thought of the books when he returns them.

Kathy knows better than we do, every time. I had picked out a Sarah Gruen novel since I liked her book, *Water for Elephants* so much. It had an attractive cover that invited a kind of quiet mystery with its Rococo design of pastels and clouds but I wasn't excited about it yet.

"You like quirky things," Kathy said. I had to agree. I mean, yes, *have you met my husband?* "I think you'll like this one," she held up a thin book (that already got my attention) with simple white letters on a red background and a faded blue clip art graphic of an old-fashioned tractor on the cover. *It's Hard to Look Cool When Your Car's Full of Sheep,* seemed like the perfect book for me. And let's face it, it came highly recommended.

What got me hooked was the back cover write-up that started, "For years people have been asking Roger Pond if his book was finished yet."

I had a running commentary in my head that went kind of like this. "Well, no…if you're close enough to ask, you would already know that if it was, Roger would be driving all over town with a box of books on his back seat finding any way to bring up the subject that his book is finally finished and ready to buy…duh!"

Which, of course, isn't the case. Because I imagine Roger is a lot like me and would not try to sell his book to everyone he knows because that is annoying. The last thing any writer ever wants to be is a salesperson.

As Kathy expected, I have really been enjoying Roger Pond's book about farm life. It just goes to show that good writers can make any subject funny and interesting to people who know nothing about their subject matter. It also goes to show that you don't have to end up on the *New York Time's Best-Seller List* to be a good writer. In fact, your book doesn't even have to be read by anyone to make you a good writer.

Roger has given me my focus back. Running around trying to get kids interested in learning a new language is noble. It has given my life a purpose. Being present, having the ability to show up consistently to school and love kids through discipline and compassion is all well and good. But my true calling is sitting in front of this little keyboard.

At this point, I am only on chapter twelve and some of the previous chapters are not fully fleshed out. The book's cover design is still in my head. We haven't had anyone to take the picture yet. But it is still my reality. My series might not make it to any *Book Review* sections but it is still my calling and I had better get to it. I have a renewed epiphany; writing is and always will be my rudder.

I feel excited again. I can't wait for Mike to come home from work. We will make a fire by the river and we will eat our baked beans out there, as we fend off mosquitoes and black flies with the smoke and our battery-operated bug zappers. It will be light enough out so that I can read my new chapter to him and then later on, I will ask him to read to me an essay or two from Roger Pond's book about farm boys playing basketball in their barns. He will enjoy reading how they sharpen their skills by jumping hay bales and dodging various types of shin-denting tractor attachments.

I think he will be happy to see that my new read has done its job of setting me back on course.

INDIE PUBLISHING

There are probably a lot of good things about being picked up by a big publisher. But I can't think of any right now. For one thing, there's a contract you have to sign, a lot of important decisions to make that involve the possibility that you might make it big some day and you have to protect your offspring so they get royalties. I'm sure that would be great problem to have but I am content with the small way things are going right now.

The truth is what a writer wants to do more than anything in the world is just write. If you sign on with someone and make it big, you have to be available to promote your book. You have to schedule interviews and flirt with media folks so that they notice you. Stuff like that doesn't really interest me.

Indie publishing isn't just about control, however, it is about responsibility. A writer is responsible for every grammar error or repetitive idea in her books. To put it another way, *the book stops here.*

The way I see it is there is no one pressuring me if my book isn't selling. With the way that new publishing works, I do not have to buy a run of books and then try to peddle them out of the back seat of my car. If someone is interested in my books, they can go to Amazon and read a sample. Then they can order a book if they want to or can download a digital version. They can even borrow it for a reduced price. You probably already know most of these things since that may be how you received this copy you are reading now.

Another interesting fact about indie publishing is that readers can live just about anywhere in the world and still have access to my book if they are interested.

The internet has changed the way that writers write and publish. It is a Brave New World, but not as dystopic. Some people may ask if this doesn't create a whole load of bad books out there. My answer is yes. But, who cares? If you are given an opportunity to sample a book first, you can judge for yourself whether you are willing to overlook some of its inadequacies. Bad books are a form of entertainment all their own, much like those B movies we used to watch.

It takes a lot of work to go the way of indie publishing but the payoff is good (I'm not talking royalties here, but could be someday). If you have something positive to add to other people's lives, it is an honor to be able to reach them. Writing may seem like a selfish endeavor but if it is, there will not be too many people willing to read your work. If done right, it is a way to serve others. Keeping it small keeps the service aspect in focus and I like that.

13. Trail Angels
July 30, 2017

I have noticed that most people up here spend a lot of time either getting through winter or getting ready for it. That's one of the reasons why we love having company during the summer. It makes us stop all of the work and helps us focus on playing. During the winter we find ourselves thinking about who is going to visit in the summer and what we might do when they come.

That's why when our good friends Brooke and Lisa came to visit, we decided to go on a favorite hike that connects to the Appalachian Trail. Mike and I would like to hike this favorite trail more often and expand a little to hike some of the AT. It is one of the reasons why we decided to move to this part of the country. The AT is not far.

The only thing is that, between building a house and building a new life, we have not been able to find a way to set aside time for that dream. It is one of the nagging things about being so full of life, you just can't possibly get to all of the things you want to do, unless you are patient. Or, you get company.

I like hiking with my friends. Conversation just seems to flow when you are concentrating on your feet. It is a lot like driving with a friend. There is no pressure to make eye contact because you have to keep your eyes on the road. I don't know why it is that keeping your eyes busy tends to help your ears stay more open.

Company reminds us that we don't really need a lot of equipment to finally get out there and play. Lisa arrived with one pair of tennis shoes and Brooke had a pair of good water shoes. She brought one pair of black jeans and some black yoga pants. Brooke wore his ubiquitous khaki travel vest (the kind that photographers use to carry a variety of lenses). You can always borrow anything you don't have when you are traveling. It is just another way to experience the terrain.

So, off we went, to our favorite trail. (Just as a side note: out of respect to my neighbors, I cannot reveal the name of this trail since they don't want way too many people visiting it. The thing is, we don't have guard rails and caution signs and all of the other trappings that come with a heavily traveled natural attraction. So, you will just have to discover it on your own.)

Lisa borrowed a lined wind breaker and Brooke stuffed a bottle of water in one of his vest pockets. He outfitted his other pockets with a handful of cherries for Lisa. They were excited to discover new territory.

On the way to the trail, we talked about the dream the four of us have had about hiking parts of the Appalachian Trail. I think it is one of those things that almost all American youth dream about doing. The AT is as much of the American fabric as Route 66 is. It is the idea of packing light and seeing what's out there. It is about meeting new people and the adventure of doing without. It is about wearing your favorite vest, sharing equipment, and being yourself. There is something about the consistent sweat that makes a decoction of who we are. There is no energy for pretense when you work the body to its end. The shedding of unnecessary layers tends to expose our truths. The consistent grit of sleeping outdoors burnishes our skin.

Since we are not currently in the position to set aside some months to hike the whole AT, Mike and I have talked about hiking parts of it. We even invested in two good packs that were fitted to us. But the honest truth is, we have not had the time to even practice using them.

"I want to be a trail angel," I said in the car on the way over. It seems to me that since I am a little grounded at the moment, I can participate in the AT from that vantage point. It is safe and comfortable and does not require anything other than a little planning.

"What's a trail angel?" Lisa asked.

"It is someone who leaves little caches of treats on the trail for the through-hikers. You leave little signs letting them know there is a cache up ahead and then the hikers find a sealed box with homemade cookies and stuff for them."

Both Lisa and Brooke liked the idea. They are the giving types. She is a regional director for Habitat for Humanity in South Florida and he is a special education teacher.

When we got to our trail, we discovered that there were several through-hikers on the trail as well. We couldn't help but engage in a little conversation with each of them. Questions about when they started, where they are from, and how long they plan to stay on the trail are pretty standard. Things became a little more interesting when we met Erin and Gary since they were from Florida too.

I asked Erin if they got some nice hospitality at Abol Bridge. It is a campground where a lot of ATers congregate to provide meals and company for the through-hikers in the summer. It is a tradition that through-hikers have come to count on if they begin their journey on Mount Katahdin. They will likely find a little barbequing going on at Abol to refresh their energies and encourage their spirits.

"Oh yes!" Erin said. In order to appreciate the enthusiasm with which she said this, you have to know that Erin probably doesn't weigh more than ninety pounds soaking wet and with shoes on. "The only thing is that they charge you to use their wifi up there and then charge for every minute of phone service. I couldn't afford to call my mom up there."

Mike, who has a soft spot for folks who look like they could use a sandwich said, "Hey, would you guys like some barbeque chicken? We have a whole bag of it."

I was confused because even though he loves helping people, he's not always the most eager to share his food. It is partly because I am not a consistent cook. There have been entire weeks where my idea of dinner might be opened bags of chips on the kitchen counter. No dip. Nothing extra. Just chips.

"Here. you might want a little salt too." I reached into my bag before Mike could change his mind about the chicken. I pulled out some potato chips and a zip-lock bag full of our dehydrated bananas.

Erin's eyes were wide and perhaps a little watery. "Meat!!!!!" was all she said. Gary smiled too.

"Hey, listen," I said, "if you give me your mother's phone number, I can text message her that we met you on the trail and that you will call when you get better service.

"Why don't you take a picture of them?" Lisa suggested.

They both smiled. Of course. When your daughter is out on an adventure, there is nothing more reassuring than a picture of her after she was just given a bag of chicken. If she has just eaten another meal of dehydrated pasta and cheese sauce, the image isn't quite as impressive, I'm sure. There's a certain radiance that comes from knowing you'll be eating soon.

We took the picture and went on our way. I knew I would not have service until I got to the main road so I saved the phone number under "Hiker's mom" in my phone. I did not want to lose it after we promised to send the text. That would be disappointing for all of us.

When I did send the message, I got an immediate response, "Thank you!!!" With a big smiley face emoji.

"You are welcome," I said. "I have two daughters in their 20's."

"(Emoji smiley face)" was her answer.

I thought about deleting the "Hiker's mom" from my contact list but I might just keep it there. Maybe one day, sometime in October or November, I might text her again, and ask how her daughter did.

There certainly is no shame in cutting an AT trip short and coming back to it another time. The trip is a heck of a strain on a human body and mind. Injuries happen. Friendships are suspended. Life at home pulls us back. But something about the way that Erin looked and the few things she said during our meeting makes me feel convinced that she and Gary are going to make it the whole way.

Maybe it was the way that they accepted help from others and the fact that they were happy that there was enough chicken to share with the loose group of travelers they were moving with.

I can't be sure but I imagine that if we start out knowing how to look for the trail angels along the way, we are more likely to make it through. Trail angels might not leave a sign or even set out to leave treats. They might just be day-hikers who brought too much food and are happy to lighten their loads. Any way it comes, if we're open to the gifts that flow in the Universe and we travel light, we usually end up getting nice surprises.

SPRUCE TIP SCONE

One of our favorite treats is scones. When you add spruce tips to scones, you have something otherworldly. The flavor could transport you to the deep northern woods and is especially good when you could use a boost.

First, you have to gather the spruce tips. Those are the light green buds that appear in the spring on the end of spruce trees. We happen to have a lot of them up here. You could use a similar recipe with other fragrant and edible tips like cedar or lavender. The key is to use the tips because they are tender and potent.

You take the fresh buds and blend them up in a food processor or blender with about a cup of sugar to 2 cups tips. You can store this sugar paste in your freezer for use at any time as an additive to any tasty treat, including pie dough or breads. I like to spread it on the top of my warm scones for a sensational presentation as well as flavor since they retain their bright green aspect. Scones are pretty easy to make. Here's how you do it. Mix together the following ingredients.

1 cup all-purpose flour (use your own mix)
3 tablespoons sugar (you can use your spruce tip sugar)
2 teaspoons baking powder
6 tablespoons butter
1 cup rolled oats (you can use quick cooking if that's what you have. Your scones will be softer)
2 beaten eggs

Your mixture should be really sticky. Just dust your hands, work surface, and rolling pin with flour when you work with it. Roll it out so that it is at least 7 inches in diameter, sprinkle with spruce sugar. Cut it into triangles and bake until golden brown at 400 degrees for 10-12 minutes.

14. Dubbin'
August 4, 2017

No matter where you live, maintaining a restful spirit is the key to joy. When it comes down to it, I owe Mike's untroubled heart a lot of credit for my happiness. Mike possesses the ability to travel light. He can cut through the absurd negativity of life, stare it in the face, and then say something that makes it all very funny.

All humans inherited the *grumpus* gene, but in Mike's case it is a recessive one. It only shows up when he feels taken advantage of or when the childhood chord of abandonment is played, but it is rare. It also surfaces when Hermes chases our visitors' cars, barks at friends, or gets into the garbage. Usually all three of these happen at the same time. I guess dogs have a form of *grumpus* gene too.

Mike is always busy doing something for someone else. That's how we built our house. He got busy building a sanctuary for my soul (and his) by the river and he stays busy maintaining it.

I think that is how he is able to maintain his untroubled heart too. His ability to squeeze out every last drop of goodness serves him well. Of course, that goodness ends up being appreciated wholeheartedly by me and those who know us. That goodness creates bonds in our community that are strong and fluid, very much like the kind of caulking that we use between the logs of our house. It never gets dried and brittle, even under extreme conditions. That's good, because we have extreme conditions, for sure.

This summer, we decided to close in our front deck with a lot of windows. We also decided to place the front deck back on the house. In typical fashion, Mike pondered and calculated. He looked at the house and determined that the south-facing front room would serve as a buffer and heat the house in the winter with passive solar. In the spring and summer, it would be a great place to dart out of the clouds of black flies and other pests. Of course, it helped that Larry had some windows he wanted to get rid of. There was no way we would have had the budget for that kind of construction if we had to buy new, or even buy them used.

It took Mike a few days of pondering to figure out how he was going to remove the old round posts from the original porch without letting the roof sag. A few things might have made it easier. One would be if he had ever done that kind of thing before and two, if he had had an extra pair of hands to hold the other ends. (He did it all while I was at work.) Too many things could have happened that would have caused a disaster. So he had to really think things through and come up with plans a, b, and c (with d just in case). He also had to build whole wall sections so that he could slide the new flat posts into place while keeping in mind the gap which would eventually closed up by a tile floor.

From my perspective, with the simple help of ratchet straps, the car jack, and some two-by-fours for bracing, Mike manages to do just about every impossible feat and makes it look easy.

He often reminds me of that Latvian man, Edward Leedskalnin, who built the Coral Castle in South Florida, on the way to the keys. This man built a dwelling and elaborate garden out of coral rocks, some of them weighing more than a ton. According to Edward's accounts, he did it all for the love of a woman who never even wanted to see it. She was, apparently, not interested in leaving her family behind and traveling in a ship from Eastern Europe to live in a rock castle in Southern Florida with no screens. When Mike and I visited Coral Castle with his mom and a friend, I couldn't help but think that if Mike had been in charge, the dwelling would have been a little more comfortable.

Doing the impossible is an almost daily activity for Mike. The first time our guests enter the house, they usually look up and sigh or say, "Wow!" Admittedly, it is impressive to see the bones of a building, like you do in a log cabin. But, the truth is, unless you have built a house yourself, you cannot really see everything that goes into constructing it.

I think that is why most people would never consider building their own homes. The complexity of it is mind-boggling. For us, it was, and is, our only option. That is why we had to keep it as simple as possible. But even so, there are considerable layers that go into building a permanent shelter.

Construction takes more than good equipment. (In our case, that isn't even one of the elements.) It takes a lot of advanced planning and research. It takes thinking and rethinking. When we have a project to do, the first thing Mike does is lay in bed. It doesn't matter what time of day, if he has a moment, he is going to lie down.

To anyone visiting, that form of "getting busy" doesn't look much like getting busy. That's why when guest season and construction season overlap, things can get a little funny, especially when our company is my parents. I see both sides. But it becomes incumbent that I explain to them that Mike is not being lazy, leave him alone, he is *thinking.*

It is human nature, I guess, to see the world through our own eyes. But seeing the world through someone else's eyes is even better. Adopting a *live and let live* attitude, even when it comes to your in-laws is, during construction season, a matter of survival. Things need to get done. It has to be now. We have no need for energy drains like having to explain every behavior, gesture, or tone.

Unlike the Eastern European lady that Edward tried to cajole to live in his "castle" of rock beds and fountains of youthful fantasy, I am totally in. I am happier than I have ever been. Mike says that had Edward's "lover" been involved in building that "castle", it might have had some frivolous elements like say… a roof or some rudimentary plumbing. This could be true but it takes a lot of commitment to leave your family behind for this kind of adventuring. I just try to balance things out by convincing my family to visit me. It is a meeting of worlds when that happens. And, admittedly, we are all getting used to it.

In my family's case, it means withdrawal from their simple comforts. It means getting used to awkward coordinating of bathroom time. It means listening to the river instead of network news. It involves using a bucket to wash with cold river water and castile soap rather than half-hour steam baths with specialty shampoos. A river bath will most likely take a couple of hours or more. It is a definite change of pace but it might not be their idea of a relaxing vacation. Getting used to having time is not always easy.

For us, time is absolutely our most valuable commodity. Up here we have a term for sitting still and doing nothing. It is called *dubbin'.* It can describe a scene like a group of men leaning on the tailgate of a pick-up truck for half a day. It could be someone just sitting in a rocking chair on a screened-in porch or sitting by a lake with a fishing pole. Up here, it is an important part of life.

And so, even though it is guest season and construction season, Mike and I might need to spend half of the morning just *dubbin'*. We spent the whole winter waiting to do just this. It is a summertime must-do and we see no reason to give it up.

We have worked hard to get to this point of doing nothing and we take it seriously. If there is one thing that Mike and I have learned about our relationship, it is that we are both such givers that we have to protect each other. He would do anything to please me, even give up his hard-earned dubbin'. It just would not be right of me to ask him to do that. I also might get so accustomed to dubbin' that I forget about planning for dinner or keeping ahead of the laundry.

These things happen, but it never is the end of the world. Forgetting about dubbin' could be, though. It could be the end of our world of peaceful hearts. And then neither construction nor guest season would happen.

If I get a chance later, I think I am going to borrow my friend's wood-burning kit and make a sign that reads:

I'm *dubbin'*.
So when you ask me what I'm doing today and I say
nothing, it doesn't mean I'm looking to do something.
It means I'm doing nothing
and I'm not quite done doing it.

THE BEAN HOLE

As far as I understand, the idea of a bean hole originated with the woodsmen of old up in the "county" (that would be Aroostook County, the seat of the North Maine Woods). It's a great way to set everything in a pot and forget about it until it is done.

It took a creative cook to feed a slew of very hungry men every day with a few dry ingredients that won't go bad and wood for fuel. Add to that the fact that a cook might have to pack up and move his operation every year. So, the simpler things were, the better.

Hence, the bean hole. It is not a new idea. Coming from the Caribbean where they jerk chicken, I know burying food to cook is a method used around the world.

The concept is pretty basic. You dig a hole big enough to loosely accommodate a good heavy pot with a tight-fitting lid and build a fire in it. You feed the fire for a few hours and then let it burn down to coals for another few hours. When the coals are live (burning red-hot), you lower the pot into the hole, cover it with dirt and the sod you dug up. Allow to bake overnight and dig it out at least a half-hour before serving.

Here's what you put into the pot. Of course, you can put anything you want into that pot. I think I might make a paella in our bean hole when we have our team party. Anything that takes a lot of time to cook, like say, beans, will work.

For beans, put soaked dry beans into your pot with enough water to cover them. Place in your seasonings, onions, and any meat you would like to cook with them. Keep in mind that the meat will be cooking for several hours in the bean hole so put it in raw.

When your coals are ready, you lower the covered pot into the hole, cover and let sit overnight. They will be ready to go in the early afternoon of the next daywhen the troops come back hungry.

Mike invented a super bean hole for our fire pit area. It is his nature to try and improve on anything that has been done before. So, he dug a hole big enough to accommodate three layers of brick around the hole. He noticed that people used bricks for their cobb ovens and kilns, so he figured that they would hold the radiant heat better than our soil. He reasoned that the clay would take a lot longer to heat up and would not hold the heat the way that a sandy or rocky soil would.

He used sand to set the bricks into place, starting with the outer layer and moving inward. The really cool thing Mike did that I'm pretty sure no one else has thought of doing is, he lowered an old stainless steel washing machine drum into the hole so that the fire has an even surround to capture and radiate heat back into the pot. That steel drum has holes in it so some heat does escape to the brick surround. It is easy to clear out any ashes after the beans are done or before the next batch and the pot fits perfectly in its little stainless steel home. It is also easy to tell when the coals are ready because the drum is red hot also.

The beans come out perfect every time with a smoky yet, somehow clean, flavor.

15. Town Meeting
August 7, 2017

Change is inevitable. So, I guess I will start there to tell you about the Town Meeting and what changes happened as a result. First, let me tell you about our town. We have approximately 212 year-round residents in our town. They would be the ones receiving the notice that went out in June announcing that there would be a Town Meeting at the newly renovated Recreation Center across from the Town Office.

Mike had an important deadline he had to meet and wasn't going to be able to attend. I had been discussing it with my neighbors all summer long. The bill up for discussion was whether we were going to finance nine million dollars to re-pave the road. It seemed like a lot of money and the promise was that our taxes would only go up for seven years.

One of the points I had to consider is that our town, unlike most towns in the United States, always operates in the black. Our Selectmen and people like Mike who are the budget committee work really hard to keep it so, very often volunteering their own services to keep our taxes low. Wrangling over a $38 fire extinguisher is commonplace at those meetings. So, to consider taking out a loan like that, is not something to take lightly.

Another interesting variable is that our town is divided in half by a river. The only way to get to the other side is to either travel to the nearest town and cross their bridge or use the old train trestle that can seem pretty scary if you're not used to it. This fact is important because only half of the people in town actually use the road on our side. The road on the Town Offices side is a state road and is kept in reasonably good order.

After talking to various neighbors all summer long, I still wasn't sure how to cast my vote at the Town Meeting. When I walked in, Willie and Marie were standing behind a nice table with a basket of blank paper ballots and some pencils. It looked like it could have been a bake sale raffle the way the table had a fresh blue tablecloth on it and the ladies had brought in some flowers to spruce things up.

Some people congregated in the back around the pool table. They brought their kids. I recognized a lot of folks I just see in passing, mostly surrounded by a cloud of dust from the road. There were a lot of people from the other side of the road, Lyn (my potter friend) and her husband, Kent, our beekeeper friends (Sami Bee Honey), and others we know. Willy later tallied and claimed that three-quarters of the town showed up to vote on the road.

There were a lot of sidebar conversations about how people were going to vote. Then, the meeting began with Marie at the front with a little gavel, calling us all to order. One by one people stood up to speak. I was glad, because even though I had talked to a lot of people and understood why they wanted to vote the way they did, I had not heard from everyone. If you have ever seen the Norman Rockwell painting called *Freedom of Speech*, you'll get a pretty good image of what our Town Meeting looks like most times.

First up was George. I have a high regard for George and his wife Bev. They would do anything to help a neighbor. Bev will invite you in and make little tea cakes and beautiful little tea baskets while George will tell you about something inspirational he heard in church or saw on TV.

"First, I want to say that Bev and I live on my military pension, which as most of you know isn't that much but we get by just fine. But, like many of you, our income is fixed. Now, the last thing I want to see is raised taxes but I have to tell you that the dust from that road is just about killing me. My doctor says that the dust is in my lungs and it is wreaking havoc. You see, it even gets through your closed car windows. It's all over my house. Bev has to work day and night to keep the dust down in our house."

Then Russell (from Russell Rapids fame) stood up. "There is a road underneath the dirt road we have right now. They just covered it, thinking it would be cheaper to maintain. My problem is people go tearing around my corner, bottoming out, and a lot of times, sliding right off the road into my yard,." (I was thinking about his hunting dogs out in front of his house and winced.)

A few other people stood up in favor. Willie said in just a few sentences that she and Bucky would like to sell someday and the first thing people are going to see is the road they come in on.

Someone else got up and talked about the wear and tear it costs on his truck. He'd just as soon pay a little extra for seven years than have to replace his truck every seven with the rust damage from the calcium chloride they use to hold down the dust, not to mention all of the damage the potholes have caused his front end.

A couple of people stood up in opposition to the paved road. One lady said she moved here for the quiet and that a paved road would invite more users and motorists who would be speeding by her house, potentially hitting her chickens that sometimes make it into the road.

One who opposed said that the paved road would require more maintenance so it was going to cost the town even more. There would be no savings by having a paved road, especially the way that it is constructed: layer over layer so the runoff isn't set up properly. "Frost heaves will make it just as pot-holed a mess, only worse, in no time," he said.

These were all good points. Then it came time to vote. I had my little piece of paper filled out and folded into four in my hand and dropped it into the little white wooden ballot box.

We sat and waited. The sidebar conversations sparked up again, only this time, people were interested to know how everyone voted.

"I'm very private about how I vote," I told the person who asked. That was fine. It is true. I don't even discuss who I vote for with my husband or my family. No one needs to know. That way, my vote truly represents what I think to be best and not who had the best argument before I went into the voting booth.

We all settled in when Marie announced that they had the results. "Out of 167 votes, 163 voted for the bond for a paved road and 4 voted against."

So, that was it. The new road was started within a month and was finished by the end of October. It is smooth and there is no dust anymore. I'm not sure if I really am going to miss Russell's Rapids or the coating of dust on my car. I'm not totally thrilled with the hike in my taxes but things change.

These days, Russell's rapids are a breeze to fly by and I hardly notice if he is outside with his hunting dogs anymore. I might have been going a little too fast to wave and say hi, too.

Though you will never know how I voted, when I pass by George and Bev's house now, I think, *well, I'm glad he's not breathing in that dust anymore.* I really like George and want him to be around for many more years. I don't want Bev to spend her precious time dusting 24-7. She is a wonderful gardener and now that all of that dust is gone, she can plant flowers beds by the side of the road That is the kind of change I can handle.

MAINTENANCE

One thing that I have learned is that Maine winters are rough on vehicles and equipment. Living out here trying to be so simple has required a lot of specialized equipment like an old truck with a snow plow attached (if you read Book I, you heard about our first plow). This year we added a 28- inch snow blower that Mike uses to create pathways to the woodshed, to clear the deck, and to push out the edges.

The advantage to the snow blower is that it throws the snow out into the woods. If you just plow, you end up having to push the snow somewhere and when it snows a lot, you end up with a narrow tunnel of snow with five foot sides. That can make it tough to get in and out of your driveway. And if for any reason your car stalls in the middle of your driveway, you will likely be stuck in it until the melt in, say, April.

The only problem with the snow blower is that we have a half a mile to maintain and after a good few days of snow, it is not unusual for Mike to be out there for five hours straight. He comes back in from that with a coating of snow all over him. Picture the Abominable Snowman and you have a close image. It is not comfortable by any means. But he does not complain.

Our plans for maintenance include a snow blower attachment that you put on your ATV. We are also building a two-car garage so that he can keep all of this essential equipment out of the snow. These complicated plans should make winter a little simpler for him. We figure that his exposed time after a big storm will decrease by more than half with our new rig.

As far as vehicles go, Mike has coated the old Ford plow truck with POR, a paint that shuts out rust. He also fluid films the bottom of our vehicles to prevent the rust that ensues after running over salted roads all winter. He just does the maintenance in the fall.

Before winter sets in we make sure that any *junque* in the yard is picked up or pushed out of the way so that we have clear pathways to the woodshed and the chickens. That includes any vehicles that might need repairing, our teardrop trailer, and any other larger items that might be in the way of the push-outs.

Maintenance is not just about winter. Important summer maintenance measures that we build into our routine now is that we fill the snowmobile tank with gas and a gas stabilizer so moisture from the summer heat and condensation does not build up in the gas tank. We also might want to take the chains off of the plow truck tires so that we can use it for hauling things in the summer. (Though this year Mike decided to just leave the chains on so the plow is all set and ready to go next winter.)

It hardly seems possible that there could ever be four feet of snow on our beautiful sundeck when we sit and sunbathe in August. When I clean and pack away all of the sweaters and winter gear for the summer, I can hardly fathom how cold it gets and why anyone would need all of that wool. But it is all part of the maintenance plan of making winter a more pleasurable time of the year. All of the maintenance might sound complicated but each act is an important part of keeping things simpler when our energy levels dip and we would rather go out cross country skiing than clearing our driveway or working on our vehicles when we get a good snow and school is cancelled.

16. Heather
August 16, 2017

This has been a hard chapter to write but I think I have to because writing about things is how I deal with life. When I met Heather, I knew immediately that we were soul sisters. There was never that uncomfortable moment between us that you get sometimes when you meet someone new. I think you know what I mean. It is a moment of hesitancy about a new commitment that you might not be ready for. Maybe this new person has expectations of friendship that you just can't meet and you sense it.

With Heather, there was never anything uncomfortable between us. The first time we met, she had invited me to go belly dancing with her. For Heather, it was perfectly natural to belly dance way up here in the Maine woods. As for me, I was surprised that there were enough Maine women interested in a belly dancing class. She also invited me to practice jujitsu with her. I loved her immediately for just those two things. Here was a girl that enjoyed busting the envelope right open without even using the edge of her buck knife. And she wanted company while she did it.

By now, I am sure that you have already discerned that I am describing Heather in the past tense. I am going to have to tell you that Heather crossed over to the Place of Great Love last year. I miss her with all my heart but, somehow, like everything she did, Heather passed with complete focus and commitment.

Rather than tell you about how Heather died, I think it's a lot better that you know how she lived. And, I'm here to tell you, she didn't live like anyone else you will ever meet. She followed her passions with full intention, making no apologies for any decisions she made.

To say that Heather and her husband Glenn lived off-grid is an understatement. For a long time she lived in a yurt that they built together on her father's back forty. That was way back in the forty acres behind a log cabin her father built out of the logs he hand hewed. Her parents were part of the original Back-to-Earthers. There is no doubt that Heather came by her wild streak honestly.

When the yurt proved to be a little too drafty and buggy, Heather's father built them a tiny house with a wood stove and a loft where they could sleep. There was no running water but she had devised a water system where she could lug it in. I say she, because Heather was not the kind of woman who would just sit back and allow someone else to do the heavy lifting. Besides water, she helped her father cut and stack the firewood they used.

By far, the most surprising thing about my friend was her knowledge of every plant in the woods, fields, rivers, and coastal regions of Maine. Having studied with Susun Weed, she knew the medicinal properties and uses of almost every plant. It had been her passion since early childhood. Her parents once told me that she would make them pull over on the highway for a flower or weed that she had spotted. She always carried a little plastic bag to take home her treasure and had all variety of wild plants growing on her father's land.

Like the wildflowers, Heather seemed more delicate than she really was. Her wispy corn silk hair and petite frame belied her powerful healing strength. This is why it was incomprehensible to so many of us that she could be taken away by an aggressive cancer. She was only forty-four and it hurt our entire community that she left us.

But like the mullein flowers that are so giving and illusive, Heather had her own timetable and wasted no part of life wondering if she was on the right track. For those who do not live where mullein grows, it is an impressively tall stalk of flowers (usually light yellow or pink) with fuzzy leaves. The stalks can reach up to five feet high in some places. Mullein is a wonderful plant for a cough and makes a good tea. Some people also smoke mullein leaves if they need a vigorous lung cleanser but it is rarely recommended to use it that way.

What I find so intriguing about mullein is that it shows up whenever and wherever it wants to. You might plant some in your flower bed and next year it decides that it would rather root down by the wood pile or across the river. Mullein has a mind of its own. When it decides to show up, it is remarkable and leaves a proud and indelible brown stalk behind in the fall and winter. The dried stalk seems to point upward and say, *"Yes, I was mullein. I am gone now. You may not find me. Wasn't I absolutely the most decorative creature? Didn't you love my silky blonde crown of flowers? Remember mullein. I am a powerful healer and will bring you comfort for your most essential of human ailments: colds and coughs."*

The funny thing is that it is because of Heather that I know about mullein. She is the person who taught me about so many of the wild plants around me. She never once balked at my many questions and patiently answered them in her own quiet way. Her interest and knowledge in the world of plants was not something that she held as a commodity, rather it was a gift that she generously shared without reservation.

Any visit with Heather turned into a weed walk. Even something as singular as blackberry picking resulted in some lesson on the uses and benefits of mug wort or the gathering of checkerberries for a cool little wintergreen cordial she planned to make.

Heather and Glenn liked to show up unannounced to gather up acorns or just sit by the campfire. One time she brought a rose cordial with her that I have been trying to repeat ever since. This year I think I finally got it. Another time they drove up with about fifteen five-gallon buckets of whole grains that they were not going to use.

Mike and I still use them to make our specialty flours. We wash them and soak them a few days, then dry them out before we grind them. It is a bit of a process but is the best way to benefit from the nutrients and most of all, flavor of the red and white wheat berries they gave us.

Heather was like that. Looking back, it was almost as though she knew she wouldn't be here very long so she had better give as much as she could while here. She picked up part time jobs here and there but never had much in the way of money or transportation. Nevertheless, she always showed up with some belt or scarf that she thought I might like. Her thoughts about people always seemed to me to be giving ones.

Heather's friendship makes me think that like so many of the beautiful and useful beings that grow wild and are then domesticated and organized into little flower beds, we sometimes like to trick ourselves into believing that we are anything but wild and autonomous spirits. We are all free to leave this place when it is our time to go and as difficult as it may be for those who stay behind, it forces us to accept that there is a power greater than any human need for company.

I know I will never stop thinking about Heather, especially when I am out foraging. There will be times when I am sure she will show up in the shape of a flowering plant and say to me in a clear, fragrant voice, *"Pick me! Plant me!"*

Heather's passing had a profound effect on the way that I see health, life, and the afterlife. Before her disease, Heather was one of the healthiest people I have ever met. It seems like so much of our time and energy these days is spent on trying to outwit death. We try really hard to do the right things so that we live long and prosperous lives. We try to eat all of the right things, avoiding foods that scientists tell us will shorten our lives.

While I will continue to practice yoga and eat as many whole foods as I can, Heather's passing taught me that the true purpose of my lifestyle is to outwit life, not death. My intention now is all about maintaining a certain wildness and verve that will not be domesticated. There are things, I realize, I would prefer less than a shortened life. These are things that rob me of my true essence and that would force me to stay confined for too long a period.

But my life's pattern is not like the mullein who chooses where and when it will show up. I might be more like the oxeye daisy who just shows up and stays as long as she would like, perking up the landscape, sometimes planted but always a little wild and slightly disheveled.

Like all living things, there is always a season of rest. We might not see the same mullein return the following spring but we know it will appear somewhere. My soul sister, true to her name, is now everywhere that things are allowed to grow freely. Her spirit is unencumbered and light, spreading its beauty across the hills and valleys of the Great Expanse of Love.

HEATHER'S ROSE CORDIAL

When Heather and I first met, we knew we were soul sisters. The second time I met her was when she came to visit me for my birthday with a magical present. It was a little bottle of her rose cordial.

I tried for a few years to recreate the full and rounded beauty of Heather's Rose Cordial. Imagine the rich experience of placing your head in a wild rose bush on a warm and sunny summer day after a few good rains. Okay, pretend there are no thorns when you do this. The heavenly fragrance fills your spirit with a knowing of Goodness.

Now imagine that knowing filling your entire body with a glowing warmth caused by a half teaspoon of a deep red elixir. It takes a very little bit of cordial to warm the spirit.

The basic procedure to make a rose cordial is that you have to pack a ball jar with freshly picked rose petals. They have to be wild. The commercially grown varieties are usually hybrid for their staying power, not for their fragrance. They can be beach roses or your scruffier backyard variety. As long as they have a good fragrance, you can use them. Make sure they are not treated with any pesticides, of course.

The next part is key. I tried for a few years to recreate the subtlety of Heather's creation but I kept failing because I skipped this step and added the alcohol too soon. That simply burnt the delicate flowers.

Take your ball jar packed with fresh petals and pour a half of the ball jar up with sugar. (So, if you use a pint jar, use a cup of sugar.) Take a wooden spoon or spatula and macerate the petals and the sugar until the sugar appears fully! integrated into the mix. Place in the refrigerator for at least two weeks, macerate it an additional few times.

I have started using a good quality vodka since we could not get Everclear in Maine when we first got here. The key is to use something that will not impart too much flavor because the rose is a delicate creature. Add enough vodka to cover the macerated petals and allow to rest for another 4-6 weeks.

Strain and place in small decorative bottles. Garage sales and thrift shops usually have little bottles that are cute but seem to have no real use. Well, they did once. They either held delicate and warming cordials or hand-made rose or violet waters.

Share with a soul sister or anyone you love.

17. The Dance
August 11, 2017

Four years ago, today, we were unloading all of the materials for our house. It was raining heavily and rained non-stop for another ten days. Looking back, we realize what blind faith we had that two people who had never built a house before would be able to put a roof on a house in time for winter. We were facing the impossible that day. But we did it.

Today, Mike and I will be picking up some more cedar decking because we decided to close in our front porch and add on a sun deck using the decking we pulled out. We just need a little more decking to finish the job. If there's one thing I have experienced up here, it is that there's always something going on in building season.

In Mike's world, there is always something going on, period. Very often it is maintaining or fixing something I have broken. He says that life balances itself out when I end up looking for something he can't find. (Most of the time when he is looking for something, it is because I put it somewhere.)

The curious thing about Mike is that no matter how serious the broken thing is, he always seems to be able to laugh at me and my foibles. Don't get me wrong, he gets serious and, sometimes a little concerned, but he always manages to find joy in the moment somehow.

I have come to realize that Mike does everything with love or he doesn't do it. It is that simple.

As it turns out, love is the magic potion that helps us do the impossible. I always say, "Love built this house." Love is the superhero that comes to the rescue every time. But it is never a silent partner. Doing things in the name of love is not enough, especially if it is done out of a feeling of obligation or duty. The job might get done but there might not be enough energy left to smile at the end of the day.

Love likes a party and always invites his sidekicks, Gratitude, Joy, and Kindness. They travel as a team and get the job done, saving the world one task at a time.

I read recently that gratitude is the antidote for anxiety and depression. I heartily admit that I live by that theory. It is the singular most important thought strategy a person can use to get off the rails of negative thinking. But, what do you do about that palpable negative energy that some people just can't seem to shake?

You know what it is, it is the nemesis, Negatron, that wrecks every party with its sidekicks Judgment, Anger (however righteous), and the energy-thief, Guilt. They take on a life of their own and like to change the music and hog the dance floor.

It can be a battle for sure. The first step, it seems, is to decide that you don't like being beguiled into dancing to that kind of music. It doesn't matter how old you are, you can decide that Negatron does not have to show you how to dance.

All you have to do to find your own groove is to call on Love and his companions. Sometimes it is easier to start with the companions than to go straight to the Big Guy. It is kind of like how the Catholics and Hindus have their saints and gods. Start off with a simple *hello* to Gratitude and ask it to introduce you to its good friend, Love, if you want to get anything done.

In the mosh pit of life, Love is the guy doing the Saturday Night Fever moves on the dance floor. Everybody gives him a little room because he's just so darned cool. It might feel a little contrived and fake to try and copy Love's dance moves but that's not really dancing. We have to just learn from him and let the rhythm move through us. Let go of how we think we might look to other people, and just let it flow.

Gratitude tells us to look at the good. Even when it all might look so bad, there's always something good we can focus on. We are still here. We have each other. We have time. We have food. We have shelter (even if it doesn't have a roof yet, it will). Gratitude says to start with the simple things because when we start thinking about them, we realize how incredibly fortunate we are. When we imagine life without the plate of food on the table, we realize that a simple dinner might be the only thing that matters. Everything else is dessert and too much of that is not always a good thing.

Then there's Joy. Joy says to look around and notice the cool things going on around us all of the time. Notice the birds, the squirrels, the clouds, the stars. Listen to the sounds of things and let them help you with your smile. It works.

Joy can take a little work but even in the darkest times, Joy can be found if we look for it. There is almost nothing more important than to seek out Joy. It is a real lifesaver.

Some of us connect to Kindness. Now, Kindness is not always easy if you have not practiced it. The best place to start with kindness is to look in the mirror in the morning and say hi to that person standing there. Try not to be afraid to see what you see there. Just be kind to that image and say something like, "Hey, nice eyes, buddy!" Kindness will tell us to look into those eyes and appreciate everything they have seen. Kindness will tell you to try it on yourself first before you do it for another person. Take it slowly. No need to rush into trying to be kind to everyone else if you can't be kind to yourself.

While Negatron will frown at your attempts to just be yourself out there, Love will smile and will shake his own funky stuff. Negatron will tell you that you absolutely can't dance. It is done this way or that and you don't have what it takes. *Stop embarrassing yourself.* Love and his friends will be too busy to notice how you do it. They're simply happy you are.

It always seems to come down to a dance-off between the two of them and before you know it, the center of the dance floor is cleared away and nobody can argue that Love steals the show. Negatron just can't keep up with Love's spontaneity and freedom. His light body does things that seem impossible and he's drumming up the energy of everyone present. Negatron has his moments for sure but he will never be able to keep Love from sweeping up.

I think about this little skit every now and again when Negatron gives me the look. You know the look. It says, *You have no idea what you're doing. Who do you think you are, anyway?* You know what I'm talking about. It shows up just when you were beginning to get the courage to get out there and DO something. But Love always shows up in the other corner of the dance floor and says, *You got this!*

That's why I say that Love built this house because it really did. Love gave us the encouragement we needed to just get out there and do it even if we did make some pretty big mistakes.

And here we are, living in it. Living in the dream we had in our minds and making it even better. Negatron will have to just sit this one out.

One of the reasons most people practice yoga is to increase their joy. If you read some of my other books in this series, you know that I am an enthusiast for the practice of yoga. I really do not think that you have to be a regular in a class or follow a certain "discipline" to benefit from the practice.

A doctor once wrote that just about any physical exercise you do while concentrating on your breathing is practicing yoga. I happen to think he is right. And the opposite is true too. You can put yourself into all of the contortions and implement the stretching movements of Hatha Yoga without concentrating on your breath and it is not truly the practice of yoga.

So, it all boils down to coordinating breath with movement. When we fully exhale, it allows our bodies to inhale fully as well. Just about all of the practice of yoga is to help us to fully exhale and appreciate the moment.

A simple exercise to invite the exhale is to reach your arms straight up towards the sky and lift your gaze. This will invite a full inhale as the chest cavity is elongated and open. Allowing the arms to widen in a sweeping circle (slowly and deliberately) towards the waist on the exhale. Do this three times and then do three more, allowing the body to bend at the waist and the arms to sweep towards the ground. Remember to use your abdomen to support the lower back as you sweep the arms upward and you unfold at the waist on the inhale.

If you pause when the body is folded at the waist and the arms are lowered to the floor, pull your belly button to your spine like a punctuation mark at the end of your exhale to squeeze out any residual spent air.

Your body will love you for the three minutes you spent giving it the vital oxygen it needs and that will increase your joy. If you do it outside under a tree, your body will love you even more. A few simple breaths can be all it takes to scare the Negatrons away. That leaves you free to take Love's hand while he leads you out onto the dance floor and you can get your boogie on.

18. Mycelium
October 11, 2017

There is a lot to be said about mushrooms. One of those things is that if you happen to eat the wrong one, you can die a horrible death. This begs the question why anyone would even consider eating wild mushrooms. For us, it has nothing to do with the thrill of dancing with death. It has more to do with connecting to the earth.

Let me explain. Mike and I used to enjoy going out on 3-D archery courses in Rhode Island where, much like golf, there are foam deer and turkey set up in the woods and markers and a point system to see if you can get a good shot in the kill zone. It is also important to watch where your arrow flies so that you don't lose it in the pile of leaves around each foam animal. When you do lose an arrow, however, it forces you to really scrutinize your environment. You probably will end up shuffling through dried leaves and feeling the ground with your feet to see if you can detect the long narrow bump that is your arrow underground (or a good straight stick).

The whole process made me much more involved in the woods and my mind needed to decode those beautiful little surprises I inevitably found there. I had to know what those incredibly colorful fruits of the earth were. The vibrant spectrum of shapes and colors set on a background of fall leaves is just a feast for the eyes. A curious mind needs to know.

Hence, the journey to photograph and research what these little guys are called and how deadly they are. As it turns out, many are harmless and some are quite beneficial. Others are so tasty that it is only a matter of time before you start going into the woods just to find them. It happens. But like the mushrooms themselves, it is important to let the process of discovery be an organic one that develops over time, naturally and custom-fit to you.

There is a saying that all mushroom enthusiasts like to repeat and goes like this: *There are old mushroom hunters and bold mushroom hunters. But there are no old and bold mushroom hunters.* This is a good mantra to follow. It is also important to never trust your field guides and social media networking sites. Nevertheless, they are important resources for learning about the process of identifying mushrooms.

Mike and I follow certain strict guidelines for the wild mushrooms we eat. And even so, we had a little snafu a few months back that was a tad more than unpleasant when we did not cook a certain bolete enough. Needless to say, we won't be as careless next time and I don't think I will be eating that type of mushroom again, even if it is boiled, roasted, and fried in butter. Nope. I'm done. If you have ever had food poisoning, it is much like that, only worse.

So, cook your mushrooms and be really sure about them if you do decide to eat them.

My interest in mushrooms goes a little deeper than just food, however. I once saw a TedTalk by Paul Stamets about mycelium that just blew my mind. If you ever get a chance, check it out. Paul demonstrates how important mushrooms are to helping humans clean up their environmental hazards, kill carpenter ants, protect us from influenza, create and restore healthy soil, and could also be used to create a better fuel source than ethanol which has inherent ethical and practical problems. This unique scientist claims that mushrooms are connected through the earth for miles and miles and form an interactive relationship with both flora and fauna.

This gets me thinking. If mycelium can be connected by a root system like that and are so closely linked to us, we also can be connected (are connected) by an energetic root system that bridges all species together. Much like the synapses of our brains where the space between the nerve endings is the bridge between thoughts, the space between us is the energetic bridge that connects us all.

On a strictly human level, what if, my brain ponders, my thought could influence the thought of someone in Japan? What if, energetically, that person's thought could have an influence on someone in Spain? If that were true, what responsibility do I have to keep my thoughts positive? It is just a thought.

That connectedness that scientists are beginning to illuminate for our ordinary brains, is what Hindus, Buddhists, and Christians have been teaching us for years. We are all one. We are connected. The sum of the parts is better than the parts. It is mathematical. The microcosm of our bodies, our cells, our atoms...they are universes themselves, a sum of an infinity of parts. We exist in this universe we call a body but each moment that we exist, we are unaware of the work each cell is performing in order for us to sit and drink a cup of tea on a Sunday afternoon. The sheer number of parts all doing their parts is unfathomable.

All it takes is for one part to slip up a little. One cell gets sick and reproduces and becomes a cancer on other cells in the universe that we call a body. It creates a growth that does not contribute to wellness but contributes to sickness. That is when the organism either finds its way to survive or recycles back into the earth.

If you think about it, human society is like that. If enough negativity becomes the norm and creates clusters, the influence could become too powerful to resist, if it is not kept in check. This thought is easy to accept. Where it gets tricky is determining the exact marker for thoughts and behaviors that are detrimental to a society's overall health. Do we follow strict, traditional moral codes? The Ten Commandments? Prohibit marginal sexual behavior? Prohibit mind altering substances? Prohibit methods to kill such as guns? It gets political. It gets complex. Most of us don't mind prohibiting others from doing things we or the people we love don't engage in.

What if…this is just a thought, now… what if, while we discussed ways to "fight" the negativity, we worked on the immune system of our systems. What if, instead of focusing all of our attention on fighting the so-called negativity, we just countered with more positivity?

It may sound like I have been eating too many magic mushrooms. But, what if science could prove that Grandma was right all along…that the power of positive thinking is unstoppable. I wouldn't want to be science if they proved her wrong. What if that uniquely American optimism, the can-do attitude that Americans are so respected and ridiculed for, really is the key to survival? What if it meant survival not just for our society but human societies all over the globe? What if it also meant survival for other species as well? If we go down, is it possible that the rest of our four-legged brothers and sisters might also go down with us? And what about the six and eight-legged? What about those with no legs to run? What about the mycelium?

Maybe good old American optimism blended with a little science and a helping of philosophy might be good for us. Add a little kale and you've got a New Age smoothie recipe. Feeding the healthy cells is important while doing damage control. If the healthy cells are starved for nourishment and feel stressed and overwhelmed, they start pointing fingers at each other and start the blame game. With all of that infighting, it is only a matter of time before a system starts to attack itself. This kind of autoimmune disorder is fatal. And, completely unnecessary.

Maybe there is something to learn from the mycelium. Not everything is textbook. Things evolve organically. Odd things might pop up on occasion. Sometimes they are slimy, sometimes their colors are so vibrant that they glow in the dark. Sometimes they are deadly. Sometimes they are mind altering. They reproduce asexually but are sometimes humorously phallic. Some are fragrant while others are downright odorous. They flourish in the darker corners of the world, living off of detritus (removing dead stuff from cluttering things up).

Mycelium reach beneath the surface for each other, understand the power of their connecters, and wait for the right moment to surface to express their singularity. They teach us that in order to survive, we must not be overly bold and hasty. We must learn from others firsthand but must spend our own time in study and experience.

Mycelium teach us to connect to the earth, to look into the leaf strewn spaces and truly see the spectacle that is all around us. They teach us to walk softly in those spaces, to spring forth out of muddy patches with our best suits on and to accept that some of us are going to be humorous or slimy. But most of us are going to be uniquely, and at times, radiantly beautiful.

BLACK TRUMPET MUSHROOMS

One of the best wild mushrooms you can eat is the black trumpet. For anyone who knows wild or domesticated wild mushrooms, it is a type of chanterelle. For those of us who don't eat in pricy Five Star restaurants (I'm guessing most of us), let's just say that you can purchase these mushrooms online for $60 a pound. Yes, they are that good.

Mike and I discovered a little patch on our land that produces these delicacies. They are easy to overlook since they are the exact color of dried leaves and have a similar appearance. So, how do you discover them?

First, your nose picks up the scent when you are walking through the woods. Then, when you rustle the leaves around a bit, your eyes pick up a pattern of round shapes in the leaves. Once you identify the spot, a little more clearing will reveal a patch of little black and gray striped trumpets (like a lily without the stem) growing straight out of the ground.

Our patch is small and probably gets hit by the moose who travels that way. My friend Claudia, however, has a patch that produces baskets and baskets of the wrinkly, fragrant black mushrooms. When you encounter a harvest like that, the only thing to do is to dry them but there is no way you and all of your friends could go through that many mushrooms in a year of cooking. So, Claudia dries them and then grinds them down to a powder that she uses to make sauces.

This is a concept I have used for other fragrant and useful cooking items. Just think of your spice cabinet and you get the idea that humans have been doing this for millennia.

Mushrooms are not just about flavor. They are also about essential minerals and a connectedness to nature that humans need. I am not sure, but it may not be the kind of thing that requires the Internet and $60 plus shipping.

19. Self Reliance
October 14, 2017

Please excuse me while I indulge in a little personal history. According to my mother's account, my parents were so poor that in order to pay for my birth, my mother agreed to make it all a spectacle. I was born in a doctor's theater. Who knows what probing and prodding went on under the florescent lights of a class for medical students when I took my first breaths?

My father was a graduate student at UCLA but, for whatever reason, he had to move on six weeks after my birth. According to the story, my parents had just enough money for the train ticket and one meal a day which they shared with my three-year-old brother.

We moved a few more times before settling into a neighborhood in New Haven, Connecticut. Looking back, I realize that it probably wasn't the best place to raise a couple of latch-key kids. My brother was in charge of feeding me breakfast and walking me to kindergarten.

We had our share of bumps and bruises but one that left a mark was the Christmas of Disappointment. A child's memory omits connecting information. But I do remember that I desperately wanted an Easy Bake Oven for Christmas and feeling incredibly disappointed that Santa did not put it under the tree for me that year.

There was no way that my father could ever understand why I was not excited to see the little plastic red teapot he had hidden in the branches of the Christmas tree for me. I am sure that he tried really hard to make me understand why Santa knew it was the right gift for me. I am sure I cried that day.

My brother and I attended six different elementary schools. While our parents struggled with trying to establish our father's career, we sometimes lived with grandparents and friends. The transience did not stop for us in middle school. We both learned to accept, accommodate, and adjust. We were the ultimate chameleons. We were good friends and kept each other company. We were consistently teased and for being new and different.

Our parents' inability to settle taught my brother and me to never settle either. It taught us to be good friends instead of enemies who constantly fight for attention. Being my brother's friend taught me how to run with the boys and laugh when I fell down and hurt myself. That came in handy while we were building our house.

Being consistently teased taught us both that no matter where we go, we fit in because we really don't have to. It taught us to have compassion for others, especially those who are new or different. We know how it feels and we know not to make others feel that way. The experiences gave us the confidence to know that we are all human and we don't have to keep up pretenses because ultimately, it doesn't matter how others see you, it matters how you see yourself.

Our parents couldn't afford junk food, flashy toys, or colored TV. They never pampered us. We went to school sick because there was no one to stay home with us. Being sick just was not an option and our mother told us so.

Our parents could not give us much, but as it turns out, it was the things they did not give us that were the most valuable. The mark that the Christmas of Disappointment left was a check mark for me. It was a lesson that taught me to never trade in my father's simple expression of wholesome love for the empty promises of some commercial. I would never again trade in pure simplicity and truth for some flashy complexity that would eventually steal my joy.

As it turns out, the best thing our parents never gave us was excuses. If we were bored or did not do well in school, we only had ourselves to thank for that. They did not have time to indulge in helping us problem solve. Kids know how to learn and they know how to play. Their job was to just let us. They never analyzed their behavior because it was the way everyone parented in the 60's and 70's.

What our parents did give us is determination, self-reliance, gumption, and a healthy helping of understanding that if something is not right or to your liking, it is you who needs to change it...the *If you are not happy about something...then do something about it. It is no one else's responsibility. You take your obstacles and make something good for you. If all you have is a piece of paper, you make a*

Mike says the Abbotts will ruin you….When you add his Rhode Island accent to it, it sounds like Abbotts but it is the *"yeah..buts"* The *Yeah,buts* will ruin you. It is saying, "I know I need to do something about this but I am not willing to."

He tells his players and workers, "I don't care about the Abbotts… get rid of the Abbotts."

"These days" Mike says, "we aren't keeping up with the Jones's we're keeping up with the Abbotts. Everybody has their own *yeah buts* to blame for not getting to what needs to get done. You know the truth but you feel as though you are exempt from it because you have a *yeah..but…"*

Today's generation has no idea what mud tastes like or how to make a paper airplane. They don't know how to make lemonade from lemons. It is not their fault. They were born into a world where everything is pre-mixed.

We learned how to make a kite out of newspaper and flour, because we had to if we did not want to be bored. In the process, we learned about flying and aerodynamics…we learned that if you tied knots in the tail, it could be a shorter tail and your kite flew better. We learned that if you built a little stand in the summer, you could sell that lemonade to people in your neighborhood. There was no police officer issuing you a fine because you did not get a permit. He was probably your best customer because his beat was the neighborhood and he walked it.

Recently on social media the question was "Name something you did that kids today wouldn't understand," and Mike answered, "Work."

The Christmas of Disappointment was a hard lesson to learn but it taught me what love means. My parents let me learn it. They did not try to protect me from life's lessons. When my kids do boneheaded things, like cry over a Christmas present, I might be more understanding… or maybe not. Sometimes the best gifts are the lessons that we don't open for 30 years. Disappointment is just a small internal failure. We let situations crowd our joy. It is a learning experience that teaches us to fix our eyes on what is important in life. We might never be forced to do that if we had never felt disappointment.

Fifty years later, not getting that Easy Bake Oven for Christmas was the greatest gift I have ever received. That little plastic red teapot might not have been what I really wanted but was what I really needed. I needed the simplicity of a teapot and the little kitchen stove my father drew on the top of an old cardboard box. I needed the care he took to cut-out a little oven door in my stove. I needed his smiling face when I sang the little song about a little teapot that I had learned in nursery school.

That Christmas was a checkmark to always remember that what I really needed was my father's undying love for me. Everything else just eventually breaks and becomes useless and fake.

I am not saying to do away with compassion. I am saying do away with excuses. Growing up, most of us never even considered using something like a major disappointment, or injury to our trust, as an excuse. We processed and stored, perhaps, those feelings for our later years but in the meantime, got busy making our lives better for ourselves. We did not get caught up in the paralysis of analysis (as Mike likes to put it). We just got busy building airplanes, kites, making mud pies, and selling lemonade.

FIGGY PUDDING

When it comes to Christmas, Mike is a little kid. He just can't help paying attention to the strangest things. For instance, one year, he *had* to find out what all the singing was about.

"What *is* Figgy pudding, anyway? And why won't they go until they get some?" So, this is how we discovered one of the best treats you can make for Christmas and he makes it every year.

½ cup butter
½ cup vegetable shortening or lard
1 cup sugar
3 large egg yolks
1 cup milk
2 tablespoons rum extract
1 apple peeled
1 pound dried figs ground or finely chopped
Grated peel of 1 lemon and 1 orange
1 cup chopped nuts
½ teaspoon cinnamon
¼ teaspoon ground cloves
¼ teaspoon ground ginger
1 ½ cups dried bread crumbs
2 teaspoons baking powder
3 large egg whites, stiffly beaten

Preheat oven to 325.
Generously grease an oven-proof 2 quart bowl or mold. Set aside.
Cream together butter, lard and sugar. Gradually add egg yolks, and other wet ingredients.
 Add next ingredients except the egg whites. Fold the stiffly beaten egg whites in to mixture.

Pour into mold and place mold into a shallow pan of boiling water.

Place on the middle rack of the oven and bake at 325 degrees for four hours, replacing the boiling water as needed.

Let it cool before releasing from the mold.

Serve in thin slices. A little goes a long way with figgy pudding. Yum.

20. Hermes
October 20, 2017

With my new job, life has gotten very busy. I think the one who feels it most is Hermes since we don't get to spend as much time together anymore. When I leave in the morning, it's usually in a bit of hurry, and Hermes has to get up before he's ready to go do his business since I can't leave him outside all day anymore.

Even though he definitely gives me the look, as if to say, "Mom, are you sure this JOB thing really is worth it?" He gets up and does what I ask because, well, he's my dog and that's what dogs do.

Though on occasion he will get into the bathroom garbage and tear up any bits of tissue he has found there, for the most part, he is a good dog and I secretly do hate to leave him every day.

Hermes is also a big dog. When he gets up on his hind legs, he is as tall as I am, so we have to be careful what we leave on the counters. One morning, out of the grace of God, Mike had forgotten an important tool at home so he drove back to get it. When he got home, he opened the door to a house full of smoke and a very contrite dog. Hermes had put his front paws up on the gas stove to probably lick a cast iron pan I had left out and on his way down had managed to turn the knob on high. We all were so lucky that it lit the stove and that it didn't get stuck on the pilot.

The cast iron pan was red hot. But the house was intact and our dog was still alive.

After that, I have been much more careful about what I leave out and remove the knobs on the stove before leaving in the morning, just in case he gets curious again.

As often as I can, I take him out (or does he take me?) for a little hike through the woods. I love the way that he bounds through the woods, wagging his tail when he has found some critter's nest and the way he comes over to me when I tell him to leave the critters alone. Only once has he had a porcupine quill stuck in his nose and I was able to remove it pretty easily. I know we both got lucky on that one.

There is something so satisfying about moving through the woods or lingering by the river with my dog. I love to watch him find sticks, try to catch crawfish, and rout around trying to play with things under rocks and eddies.

Hermes never seems to age. He is just as energetic and crazy-happy to see me when I get home from work as he was his first year of life. It is probably the most annoying thing about him because he jumps all over me and anyone else who has come to visit. This behavior drives Mike mad and I don't blame him. But he is a crazy dog and I still have not been able to train him to calm down.

Hermes is a great host dog. I never have to worry about how he will behave when visitors bring their dogs with them. He is patient when other dogs eat his food or when puppies get a little too playful. He loves other dogs and when they visit, he knows his job is to show them around the woods and the river.

When we were the only ones living on our road, letting my dog roam wasn't too much of an issue since he had over 100 acres to wander. I did worry on occasion when Mike would find him across the main road where the logging trucks zip by at such a speed that they wouldn't even see him. That is when his outdoor time would be limited.

Other considerations are during hunting season. He wears a bright orange toddler's T-shirt during season, only goes out during the day during non-hunting hours, and spends a lot more time close to home. But for the most part, Hermes is a free dog. He plays with the chickens, chases squirrels, finds mice, and goes down to the river if he feels like it.

Now that there are more people on our road, I have seen his tracks going to their houses and I know he is stirring up their dogs. I know that's not very neighborly but I'm not sure how to fix it other than by putting in an invisible fence. It is one of the changes I'm not completely keen on having to make.

Summer is his favorite season. He knows when dinnertime is and hits up all of the camps around to pick up whatever the kids have dropped or the campers' dogs don't get to first. The people who have camps on the other side are all big dog and horse people so they love it when he stops by to visit. They call him The Mayor. I always know when they are here because that's the only time he will ignore my call. It is also when he is completely disinterested in dinner. It is tough to compete with hot dogs fresh off the grill.

A few times I have gone by there just to be sure he isn't bothering anyone and I will see him, completely at home, laying under their picnic table, or sitting by the fire. Fat and happy.

Larry always packs cheese for Hermes. It's his special treat. I guess that's why when Larry is up, our dog is bound to be hanging around his deck the minute he gets outside. I like that.

In the winter, Hermes likes to be inside to stay warm. That about sums up what we all like to do around here. Even though his paws get full of ice when he runs through the snow and it cracks his paws and sometimes makes them bleed, he gets very excited when he sees me strapping on my snow shoes. His favorite thing is to walk in my tracks (usually right on the tail end of my snow shoe, sometimes causing me to fall over). Walking on packed snow helps keep the ice from gathering on his paws so he can stay out longer. And coming inside to a warm house melts his icy paws so they feel better in minutes.

Getting out and playing in the snow is so much better when we do it together. If I don't have time for snowshoeing, he will usually just bound up and down the driveway Mike has just plowed and do his business where the snow is packed down. When you consider that the snow can accumulate up to five feet, it's not always convenient for a dog to break trail. He only weighs about 73 pounds but that's just enough to sink through when it's fluffy. If there is a bit of a crust, he will take his chances and skid along the top layer but it has to be for a good reason, like a winter squirrel that is eating all of the bird feed. He knows that bugs me and it is a pretty good game.

The other thing Hermes likes to do is help Mike snow blow the half mile of driveway. He likes to get snow blown all over him and then shake it off the way that dogs do. It's his winter bath. He also sometimes will squirm around in the snow if it is freshly fallen on the driveway. Those are the moments when my dog is the happiest, especially if he can shake off again in the house. He knows that peaks my interest in him and usually means I will get out a towel and give him a good rub. I think he has me pretty well trained.

It is hard knowing that Hermes has to wait for me every day to get home from school and yoga. Most days I have to get dinner ready and it is too dark to go for a walk or snowshoe, anyway. But, the restoration it gives my spirit when I do go out with him is great for us both.

I know there are a lot of dangers for a dog who runs free: things like porcupines, coyote, and logging trucks but I can't help smiling when I think that Hermes has the chance to be a free dog.

DOG FOOD

I guess most people generally settle on the kind of dog food they prefer to use for their dogs and then just go with it. (This is probably true for cats also.) I can't seem to do that. I find myself constantly reading the labels on those huge bags of dog food, trying to determine if Hermes is getting the nutrition he needs and isn't getting things his body can't process. I guess that's the mother in me.

Mike is different. He will check the contents but usually buys what is reasonably priced and also what Hermes likes to eat. That ends up being chunks of stuff shaped like little golden chicken legs, reddish-brown steaks, and green peas with words like *charbroiled* on the package. When I check the bag for nutritional breakdown, it does seem pretty comparable to most of the others, so I'm fine with it. Whatever makes the boys happy, I say. And let's be honest, he is a dog after all.

As a youngster in the Caribbean, I learned how to make my own dog food from rice, scraps of meat, and leftovers from the table. You could buy commercial dog food but it would cost more than the dog because it had to be imported.

So, when your neighbor comes by your house with a blue bin of bear his customers hunted and there are bones and scraps left over from processing the meat, the best thing to do is make dog food from it.

That's when having a good pressure canner comes in handy (again). I take the smaller bones that fit into the wide-mouthed quart jars and then fill the rest up with scraps and broth. Clean the edges and tighten the tops, place in your pressure canner for 170 minutes. It is better than any commercially canned dog food on the market, for sure. And Hermes goes crazy for it. I also know that it is full of Vitamin D and not full of chemical additives, sterols, coloring, and whatnots.

If you don't happen to have a neighbor who brings over a blue bin of bear, I am sure you can think of plenty of ways to make this idea work for you. Just a simple bone broth can boost up the dog bowl. Heck, it could boost up our own bowls too. Broth used to be something that was always on the backburner. When you have your own dog food on the shelf, giving your dog a good, healthy treat every now and again (or consistently) takes health off the backburner and makes it a little easier. (And economical, I might add.)

21. Teacherman
November 22, 2017

Last week our little school of less than 500 students, grades 5-12 lost a teacher. Though he had his health issues, Dave's passing sent a category seven seismic wave throughout our little town and much beyond. Dave had been a science and math teacher in our school for more than thirty years. That fact alone is worth a bit of research.

The title of the paper could be something like, "How a human could summon up that much stamina in a lifetime." The research is still inconclusive on whether that kind of longevity is possible anymore. They just don't make them like they used to. Or is teaching not like it used to be? I'm not sure. But in the petri dish of today's small school, the science is still out. Getting young people to want to become teachers is getting harder and harder.

But, let's get back to Dave. I might not be the most qualified to write about Dave since I only knew him a little over a year. However, he was my mentor so I got to have some meaningful conversations with him about the profession and how he viewed his place in the world of service.

Beyond the amount of time Dave put into his job is the fact that he saw himself as an important figure in kids' lives. He never downplayed how important it was that he was in his classroom early every morning, taking no guff from anyone, but giving his heart and mind to any kid who needed him. He teased kids, noticed what they were wearing, if they had been cold the night before, or if they had eaten enough over the holidays.

Dave loved Christmas and made no secret of it. He decorated his room every year and always lovingly took out his crèche right after Thanksgiving. It had a special place behind his desk. The last time I saw Dave, he was meticulously repairing a ceramic Christmas tree a student had given him years ago. It had practically shattered when it fell off his desk and he had already put in a few hours gluing tiny pieces together. It was still there on his desk when his family came to retrieve his personal items. All substitutes knew not to move anything on Dave's desk. An unknowing soul might have easily mistaken his recent project as a pile of refuse and jostled, or worse, thrown a piece out in a well-meaning attempt at helping him clean up.

Knowing that kids might be cold or unfed on Christmas deeply bothered Dave. He invited kids to his house for Christmas dinner and rejoiced when they slept soundly in his Lazy Boy recliner after gorging themselves on turkey and stuffing.

Dave knew what his mission was and he never wavered in his execution of it. He feared no accusations because he knew his intentions were true. He cared about kids and would have adopted every one of them who needed a safe home. He even tried to get the school district to buy a building for kids who needed a safe, warm place to live where there would always be enough food.

Dave was aware of our kids' circumstances because he took the time to listen and care. But he also demanded their attention when it came to math. There was a non-stop parade of reluctant morning faces in his room; many of them were repeats. Dave could simultaneously give a new teacher advice, direct a student as he worked out his problems on the board, and beat himself at solitaire on is computer. And though he hardly left his room, once he opened his door and turned on his lights, he always knew what was going on in school.

He knew which students spent the night in the cold, which were acting out, which were reaching for warmth in the wrong places, and which were trying so very hard just to be in his room working on their math homework. He loved and respected them all because he understood that life isn't fair, it's what we are given, but a teacher's place is to teach kids that they can be better than their circumstances.

Dave's eulogy might have been a little disconcerting to anyone who doesn't understand that kind of teacher. It was given by a former student who became a friend, a beautiful young blonde who spoke of picking Dave up in her old car for morning coffee talks and the way that he mentored her when her father died. Everyone who knew Dave and knows that kind of teacher, understood completely why his wife Gina thought this to be the most fitting eulogy for her husband. It was also telling of the type of wife she has always been.

You can't love that kind of teacher and not expect some of his students to show up for dinner or at least take up the lion's share of dinner conversation every night. Those are the reasons why you love him so much. With him, you become part of this greater love that is a lifeline to so many who, more than anything, just need to be loved.

It is a simple equation. The only problem is that there are still a handful of teachers who mix up the variables and use their positions of power to exact their own sick desires and hold everything but love and respect for kids. These are the deplorable ones, the ones who make it hard to be a true, good teacher like Dave was. When some of us get the wrong answer, it does not mean that the test is wrong.

These aberrations make it hard for the rest of us to see a kid shivering on the street who could really use a warm ride to the library where he can thaw out while he plays his videogames. Legality and caution dictate over our hearts as we zip past them on our way to our own comfort zones. The reality is that we don't possess the gravitas that over thirty years of a good reputation can impart. No new teacher does.

So when a town loses a teacher like Dave, it is like losing the enormous oak on Main Street. The landscape is stark and cold. There's nothing to break the bitter wind from robbing any warmth we can muster up and winter is coming.

What is remarkable is how in a small community like this, we all do our best to cover the kids. Our veteran middle school math teacher stepped up to the high school to take care of the kids who are graduating in the spring. Now the honors and AP track kids can keep up the rapid pace that they were accustomed to in Dave's classes. There's no time to wait and see if someone will apply for a high school math position in the middle of the year in a rural school with so many needs. It is no secret that good teachers are getting harder and harder to find in the best circumstances.

Our "new" math teacher is working with the only other veteran high school math teacher, teaching their own classes and Dave's classes at the same time in what can only be termed "triage." She is entirely aware that she leaves a bleeding wound in the middle school so that she can attend to the heart. It is not the best for her as she moves out of her comfort zone in the last few years of her own 30 plus teaching career, but she knows it is the best for the kids.

Not being able to fully understand what she has given up for them, the kids are not always the most gracious. But, eventually they will understand that what a teacher gives is so much more than just lessons in math or science; a teacher gives completely and selflessly of her mind, heart, and soul every day.

No time does that fact become more apparent than when we lose a teacher like Dave. The lives he helped guide and the kids he saved number in the thousands. The little church where he worshipped on the hill about a quarter mile from school was busting at the seams on the day of his funeral.

That day, students reached for hugs, knowing that the great big bear who protected them all as long as they showed up to his room, would have to protect them in other ways now. For those of us who are left behind, it means reassuring them that life does go on, that expectations will still be high for them, that they can mourn his loss but they must focus on the knowledge that they once had a teacher that good. They must be taught to be kind and generous in spirit to the teacher who took over for him. They must be given room but not an empty one. The room we give them must be filled with chalkboards and challenges, Christmas lights, student projects, plants, old student gifts, and maybe an occasional game of solitaire.

BISCOTTI

Dave and I used to talk food sometimes. As are the plans of mice and men, I had planned to surprise Dave and his wife Gina with some homemade biscotti for Christmas. Being Italian, he told me that he loved it but said that he saw no reason to make it when you can buy it.

My experience with store-bought biscotti is that it is dry. That is why I thought he might enjoy some fresh homemade varieties. It is really not that complicated and is well worth the time.

So, here it goes.

1 cup whole almonds
2 ¼ cup flour (you can really creative here and even use almond flour or other mixtures)
1 ½ teaspoon baking powder
½ teaspoon salt
½ cup sugar (you can play with this, as well)
¾ cup brown sugar
3 large eggs
½ cup olive oil
1 tablespoon almond extract
½ teaspoon vanilla extract
1 teaspoon lemon zest

Roast your almonds either in a cast iron pan or in the oven. Mix together the dry ingredients. In another bowl mix all of the wet ingredients. Mix both together. Line a baking sheet with parchment paper. Divide the dough in two. Make two long logs. Use damp fingers to shape the dough into a log shape. Sprinkle the roasted almonds on top. Bake for 30 minutes at 325. Remove the baking sheets and slice logs about ¾ of an inch thick. Place the slices back on the cookie sheets and bake again for 15-20 minutes. Place on a wire rack to cool. The more you bake them, the drier they get and the longer they will last.

You can add anise, orange, chocolate, or anything else you think might work. Have fun and make sure to share with a friend. Dunk them into some good coffee or maybe a little wine and be merry while you can.

22. Stars 2
December 15, 2017

Mike and I often joke that we are like binary stars. We revolve around each other, each one with as much gravitational pull as the other, keeping us in a nearly impossible state of togetherness. If it did not exist in the Universe, we might not have so much faith in its power. But binary stars do exist out there. We have our example in Nature. We can believe.

Sometimes I wonder what would happen to my star power if somehow we were separated but that is far too much to think about right now. For some reason, only known to the great mind of Nature and God, we are linked together in our orbital journeys and the result is mighty.

Every now and then, someone might ask me how I could possibly do so much and I can't help but think that it is entirely due to my twin star. We join our forces and ask the heavens to see fit to help us in whatever the endeavor is at hand.

When a situation requires a little more energy on one of our parts, the other person steps in to give support. It is not just the clichéd moral support that you might think. It is the real get-in-there, get your hands dirty (or dusty) kind of support that we give each other. We have been doing it so long that we don't even notice how we do it.

The gravitational pull that keeps us aligned might show up on a tough carpet job to help scrap up and put tools away. It might be wearing a tweed skirt and tall black boots but it is always willing to don a pair of work gloves. It might also show up on an early afternoon to help make popcorn for the sophomore class fundraisers, to sit in the audience for the talent show, or wear a silly Mexican sombrero for a Spanish skit.

No matter what the two of us are doing, we are probably laughing while we are doing it. And, as long as it is helpful to someone, we will always assume that the other person is going to be there for back-up. We never have to ask if it is okay. We just know that the other star will be there with a can-do attitude and an awareness that *help* means not asking what needs to be done. Help just knows and does it.

I guess I don't have to look any further than the house we built together to understand what that kind of power means. Together we can do hard things and keep doing them.

But like our namesakes, the binary stars hold both an imminently stable and a tenuous relationship to one another. With the slightest shift in gravitational pull comes disaster. The two stars will eventually collide if their powers are not evenly matched. That kind of imbalance must take a few eternities, if not more. I can only guess because I am not an astrophysicist and can hardly even spell the word correctly. But my poet's mind still makes the connection. An imbalance in gravity is disastrous when you get that close to another star.

To a realist, like Mike, this means that one star must never try to steal away the power of the other. This takes a constant awareness since it is so very human to want to manipulate others to pump up our own powers. It is built into us to try and diminish other people's power so that we can boost up our own serotonin. It is how tribes get leaders. They need these alpha types to keep them from sitting around and discussing where to hunt instead of just hunting.

So, making sure that the powers are balanced between the stars means to give credit where it is due, look to the merits of the other person rather than the faults. For us that means embracing the other star's faults and realizing that even stars are imperfect lumps of matter without the fire. In short, we try not to steal the other person's thunder because that's just not cool.

Mike puts it this way, "By its very nature, one person cannot take the power from the other person. The other person's light is just as important for you. If you build up their light, it builds up yours and you stay in balance. If you steal the other person's light, you'll crash and burn, get flung out into space with nothing but the clothes on your back and almost no friends." That's bad.

But everything in Nature wobbles just a bit. We do too. There are times when we get just a little too close for comfort. Things get heated but we find a little distance, cool things off, and find a way to get back into balance. Most of the time, the mechanisms of Nature get us through. The power of attraction is infinitely stronger than the powers of force. When two stars collide, the fallout is blinding and could possibly leave a gaping black hole that sucks for everyone.

Binary stars remind us that in Nature, impossible things happen. The only thing that limits the human mind is its own sense of knowing. If what we know is that two people cannot stay together and support each other throughout a lifetime, then that becomes our reality.

For many of us, there is a rich generation of binary stars to look up to. My parents, my aunts, my uncles, and many of my friends are examples of binary stars that manage to keep the balance of power in their own ways.

The one thing they have in common is that they manage to be more powerful together than they would be alone. Twice the light.

WORLD'S LARGEST CINNaBUN

I'm not sure how you actually spell it, but Mike has been known to tell folks that the true meaning of life is the center of a cinnabun. I'm not sure I agree entirely but he does make a point.

So, for his birthday I made him the World's Largest Cinnabun for a cake and he absolutely loved it. The coolest thing is that it is technically a breakfast food so I could surprise him with breakfast in bed and he could blow out his candles first thing in the morning.

That is a fun surprise. So, if you know someone who would feel really loved or needs to find out what the meaning of life is, here's the recipe. It's pretty simple.

Make a sweet dough recipe by combining 2 cups flour and one package dry yeast. Heat and stir 1 cup milk, 1/3 cup sugar, 1/3 cup butter, and ½ teaspoon salt. Heat until 120-130 degrees.

Add to flour mixture with 2 beaten eggs. Add flour as needed for a good dough texture and knead. Cover and let rise for an hour.

Melt 3 tablespoons butter (I used 4), ½ cup sugar and 2 teaspoons cinnamon.

Roll out half of your dough into a rectangular shape. Brush with melted butter and sprinkle with your cinnamon mixture.

Cut into 1 inch strips and begin rolling the strips of dough into a spiral. When you have it started, place your spiral into a greased 2" pie plate. Continue wrapping the strips of dough around and around in circles until you need to roll out the second part. Repeat instructions until the World's Largest Cinnabun is formed and is busting out of the pie plate when it has rested for 10 minutes.

Bake on 350 for about an hour. Drizzle with a cream cheese icing. When it cools, it will cut just like a cake but the center should be heaven on earth.

Cream cheese frosting:

6 oz. cream cheese
½ cup butter
2 teaspoons vanilla
4-5 cups powdered sugar

Blend until smooth.

(Like Mike would say, the meaning of life is not to sit around losing weight.)

23. Heat
December 15, 2017

We heat with wood. We do not have to buy any wood. Between helping people out with trees that have fallen in a storm and cleaning up our own acreage, we have more than enough wood to stay warm for a few years. Wood heat does require that we gather up the logs which sometimes weigh up to 100 pounds before splitting. Mike uses our wood splitter to split them. Then I usually stack the split logs in the wood shed.

We used a little over four cords of wood to heat our house during our first winter. Then Mike spent most of the next spring and fall insulating every drafty nook and corner of the house. Last spring and summer, we built a sunroom on the south side of the house and that has made a considerable difference in the amount of wood we use to heat the house.

Depending on how cold it is outside, heating up a log cabin when we have been gone for more than a few days can take several hours. Once it is heated up, all of the thermal mass radiates back into the house and keeps it warm for days. This is why we chose a log cabin construction. It is highly efficient.

Last December Mike and I found a cheap flight to go down to Florida to visit our relatives. We knew the house would get pretty cold while we were gone but we counted on the weather holding at about freezing and not dipping too far below that mark. It is just like Nature to surprise us and the temperature dipped below zero on a couple of nights. Add to that the fact that we arrived late at night so we could not monitor the wood stove closely enough to keep the temperature up and you can imagine how cold it was that night.

Fortunately, we have a buffalo robe, lots of wool, and a long shearling coat I found in a second-hand store that I keep just for this purpose. We also use a portable propane heater for these instances. It was 28 degrees inside and the bones of our house were beyond cold. The heat just could not keep up. It took more than 24 hours to get the house back up to warm. But, that was before Mike spent so much time insulating all of the drafty areas.

When we were designing what kind of house we wanted, we knew that heating it was going to be our biggest consideration. It takes a lot of effort to heat a house whether it is through oil (costs a lot of work hours) or you pay for wood delivery (also work hours, but not as many). Then you have to stack the wood in a place that you probably had to build (or have built) and go get it when it is cold outside.

It sounds like a pain and sometimes it is. But, most of the time, it is a pleasurable part of our lifestyle. Stacking wood is great exercise and bringing it in is sometimes the only chance you might get to check the stars or get outside for some fresh air.

Nevertheless, it takes work and whatever we could do to mitigate all of that effort would be worth it. That is why we chose to build a small house with an open floor plan and put our bedroom upstairs in the loft where the house is warmest. We also chose to use cedar logs with an insulation package that keeps any drafts from coming in from between the logs. The logs radiate heat back into the house while we are away at work during the day and at night when we are sleeping.

This winter, we estimate that we will be going through about two and a half cords of wood, judging by how much we have used so far. At this rate, we are saving about a cord of wood a year. That's a lot of saved effort down the road. It also results in savings if we ever have to order wood from someone else. It is a win-win.

Heat is not just a matter of comfort in Maine. It is a matter of survival. But wood heat, I have found, is a little more about comfort. The visual warmth you get from staring at the fire in your wood stove warms your cockles (that's how grandma would put it). By the way, cockles are the ancient parts of your heart that only make it into rare conversations with older folk or old souls.

My friend Quimbly claims that her father used to say that the heat from a log warms you four times. First when you cut the tree and chop the wood, then when you stack it in the woodshed, third, when you go outside to bring it in, and fourth when the people you love recognize how much effort you put into making sure they are warm.

That is how I see wood heat. When our friends like Paul and Rochelle call us because their enormous, healthy maple tree fell over in a storm and is damaging their fence, we knew we were doing them a huge favor to remove it.

We also knew that warm feeling in our hearts will last for years to come because they gave us all of that great wood. When we finally dig out that section of maple in the woodshed on a frosty winter evening, we will remember the summer when we helped them and they helped us. It is hard to get that kind of warmth from oil.

A SNOW FORT

One of the best things about winter is how clear the sky is at night. The only problem is that we end up staying indoors a lot to stay warm.

My friend Claudia taught me how to take a snow bank and make it into a snow fort that is so warm, you can stay outside for hours. The key to a good snow fort is to create a crescent shape around the spot where you will build your fire and then shovel out benches where you place spruce boughs as cushions. The best insulation under your seat is a sheep or deer skin but wool blankets also work.

The best place to start is where you plan to put the fire. Keep in mind any trees overhead. As you hollow out the fire circle, you pile the snow on the banks to add some height to the sides. You do not have to shovel out to the ground. The fire will burn just fine on a layer of ice.

When you have the fire ring all set, start to dig into the walls to make benches. If you have a metal shovel, you can use the fire to heat it up and use the back to melt the snow on the benches to harden them up a bit. Another method is to use a watering can or something similar. A light sprinkle of water will form a layer of ice on the benches so they don't sink when you sit in them.

When you have your snow fort done, you will want to invite company over to sample your cordials and star gaze with you. If you take some candles and put them in glass ball jars, you can sink them into the snow around the fort, maybe making a pathway in so that people can see where they are stepping as they approach the fort.

It is a nice way to share the warmth.

24. Time
February 5, 2018

The weather this weekend was quirky. It snowed for two days straight but it was a light fluffy snow that only builds up a little so people were in a good mood. Today it is raining so the roads are slushy and icy. It is Monday morning so the school district called for a two-hour delay. I could go into work a little early and set up my week in a slow, pleasant manner or I could stay home and write a chapter. Considering that I stayed late on Friday to wrap things up for the week and then I went and spent an hour after work helping Mike scrap up a carpet job in the local hardware store, the rest was welcome. Mike had had a pitching lesson at 10 o'clock on Sunday morning. Then we both went back to school on Sunday to help with the sophomore class fundraiser so the weekend was less than restful.

Time is precious now, and presently, I have only a limited amount of it to dedicate to writing. The funny thing is I am okay with that. I know that my mind is filled with a long, detailed to-do list daily. I know that I go to bed and wake up in the middle of the night thinking about what I am going to say to my students or what plans I will make to keep them interested. My job in a rural Maine school has its challenges but my job title is clear and I know that it is something I plan to do for a set time and when I am done, I will be better off for having done it.

I took the challenge and am meeting it on a daily basis. I am growing while my students grow. I am learning new things every day and deepening my knowledge of things I thought I already knew. School has helped me stand tall and roar like a lion. It has also helped me accept my place in the Universe as a player for Team Good.

I am content in that. I am busy and have no time for malaise. My activity has decreased my need for over concern or worry. It has given Mike and me the ability to fluff up our play money and prep up for the next phase of our life together.

Between the type of work Mike does and all of things he is able to do, and do well, there's always someone who could use a little help. As a softball coach, it is his pleasure, truly, but it does take a little time, that's for sure.

Add to the list the number of times he receives a desperate text message from a player's mom saying that her daughter can't stop crying and only he can fix what's wrong.

"She won't tell me what it is but says she can't go to practice until it's fixed. Can we do it now?"

He might say something like, "uh…it's the middle of the day… isn't she in school?"

"Yes", the mom might say, "but I need to get her to calm down. You are the only one that can help. I'll sign her out when you can be there."

"Okay, see you both at 12." And that is a story that happens pretty often. He would drop everything to see a person smile. He would and does do anything to make a person, young or old, feel happy or warm. He will finish up the emergency session with a high-five and the words, "Coach for Life!" Sometimes I can't believe that I am married to the guy in these stories but I am.

Time is what we have to give and we try to never think of it as *giving it up.* Taking time to pay attention to what people say or need is what we do. It makes no difference how people perceive you. It makes a difference if you were able to perceive them honestly and without judgment. That kind of perception takes time.

The other night Mike and I watched a YouTube video about a University pitcher who was pitching in a playoff game without a face mask and a line drive knocked her off her feet. She came back out on to the field within minutes to finish pitching the game (this time they made her wear a face mask). Mike said he thought that coach should be fired for putting her back on the mound after a hit like that.

"You don't know what kind of internal damage she has suffered. That kid would be taken straight to the hospital if she had been my player. No game is ever worth the well-being of a player."

As it turns out, that pitcher's performance during her next game was uncommonly poor; her performance had suffered because her brain had been damaged. She decided to transfer to another University where her coaches and doctors worked together to set a reasonable training plan which included no live batters for a long period of time. They were more interested in her as a person and a student than as a star pitcher but believed that she could make it back to her former status if given time.

As it turned out, her new coaches were right. Her new team won the NCAA championship in their class that year and the pile-up on the mound was impressive, though I am sure that pitcher's mother was a little nervous about her daughter's head under all of those screaming young women.

This story reminds me that while we sometimes are like that pitcher, we "try-out" for jobs or relationships and we feel a certain pressure to do whatever it takes to prove to that institution or person that we deserve their faith in us but so very often that objectifies us. We are accepted as long as we can perform. That kind of pressure can be less than productive. Everything is okay, until the pressure makes us crack and then our performance suffers.

That coach from her former university objectified his players. They are useful objects. How many of us feel that the minute we slip, we're out? What if we were approached by our bosses the same way the new coaches approach their players? What if our bosses took the time to perceive what makes us perform better, believed in us, and gave us the time to prove them right?

As busy as Mike and I have been between teaching, taking a class in contemporary Latin American literature, teaching yoga, working on a book for my father, sophomore popcorn sales two or three times a week, privately coaching pitching, and working out there on all manner of construction, flooring, car maintenance, plowing and snow removal for two families and a camp, we still take our time at the end of the day to be grateful for all of the opportunities we have to be of service.

Time is what we have to give.

CABRALBALL

As a softball coach for more than 30 years, Mike has developed some staple concepts and strategies that make him a very good coach. This is not undue pride on the part of a coach's wife. This is just an honest assessment based on objective observation. So here are some things that Mike might say or do.

Number one: you're dealing with kids so you never curse. That's why Mike has had a designated player whose job it is to curse for him when things get out of control on the field.

Getting up to bat is a big responsibility so you have to be prepared. Part of that is your thinking. First, you have to think a positive thought like, "I am the greatest batter to ever step up to plate." It might sound insincere but it replaces the negative thoughts so many players step up to bat with. The negative self-talk will undermine performance every time.

Mike wants them to be in control of their thoughts when they get up to bat. Too many times, your brain thinks, "Oh God, please let me just hit this ball," and that makes you swing at bad pitches. The brain should be thinking *where* you are going to hit it and what kind of pitch you are waiting for.

When players strike out, he tells them, "You never get mad. You never let that pitcher think she's got you. You think, *that pitcher sure got lucky.* You take note of what happened and then you tell the next batter what to look for." Getting mad just brings everyone else on the team down. Ego and pouty crying will destroy any future opportunities you may encounter. It will also destroy your team's opportunities.

Mike will tell them, "If you want the truth, ask me. Otherwise, don't." (I know this one very well!)

Mike never yells but when a player has found the limit to his seemingly endless patience, he might say, "I've had it with you. I'll just ignore you." (Trust me, you don't want to be there.)

"Once you put on those cleats – be aware of the way you walk. You want the other team to think, *Wow! We have our hands full.* We want them to worry about us the moment they set eyes on us.

"If you think outfield doesn't matter, try playing without them." That goes for bench players too. They had better believe they matter and be ready because they might have to put on the helmet during any inning. Their head has to be in the game at all times. They need to know what pitch they will look for and where they will hit the ball.

Base running is as important as any other skill. If a player has never been thrown out on a steal, he'll talk to them about being more aggressive with their base running.

When a bad call costs their team the game, he never allows them to be upset at the umpire. His response is that they should never let a game get that close. He demands that the umpires are treated with respect and that his players never question the umpire's decisions. That's his job and he does it well.

"I hate to lose but I never mind being beat." The contrary is true too. Even if his team wins but they didn't play well, he will tell his players that they didn't really win; the other team just lost.

Mike teaches his players to walk away from every situation asking themselves, "What did I learn?" As a rule, he will never bench a player after an error because it then becomes a punishment and indicates a lack of belief in that player and then she will stop believing in herself.

Mike tells his players that the most important thing is to never be afraid to fail. He tells them that they will never remember the times that they failed. But, says, that in their lives and in their games, they will make that one great play that they will remember their whole lives. He tells them, "Don't let your fear of failure prevent you from making that one great play."

Most of all, Mike teaches them that winning isn't everything but it is a lot more fun than losing. "So, let's go have some fun and respect the sport!"

Author's note: Mike was elected the 2018 Maine Coach of the Year by his colleagues for his division and his team won the 2018 State Championship for their division. It would be the first time the girls' softball team would win a state championship in Greenville's school's history (est. 1919). Now, that's worth mentioning as a good use of his time.

25. Out
April 5, 2018

I just want to make this clear from the start that I never thought ending with this chapter was a good idea. But, I'm beginning to learn that life doesn't really care about which chapter we'd like to end with.

This chapter started last week when I had a planned day off to get some routine medical exams done and the day before, I couldn't get out of bed because my Lyme disease had decided to take the show that day. See, the pesky little Lyme critters are all still inside me. They spend all year waiting for the weather to warm up to one day say, *yeah, I'm taking over today.*

For the past few years, I have managed to keep them under control, using diet and homeopathy but every now and again, my resistance slips just enough and they get bold. I am not going to bore you with all of the details of Lyme and what it does to people. But I will tell you that it messes with your head and it makes you think really dark thoughts about yourself and life. Normally I try to be too busy doing good things with my life to notice, but Lyme takes you out so you can't just *busy through.*

Even so, I decided to do it anyway. I went back to work and contracted pneumonia. I guess doubling down just doubled down the impact the bacteria has had on me. So, I've been out.

The beauty of all of this is the absolutely genuine well-wishing I have gotten from everyone I have had to contact for cancellations (like my yoga ladies who are just so loving) and the secretaries at school (also my yoga ladies, as life goes) have been incredibly helpful and caring, never once making me feel like a complete failure for not being able to deliver sub plans.

See, the funny thing about being a teacher is that YOU ALWAYS HAVE TO LEAVE SUB PLANS. And, I honestly left work last Friday thinking that all I needed was a good weekend of rest. There would be no way I would *miss a whole week of school*! I am a healthy person. That's just not the stuff I'm made of. I push through and make things happen. I am organized. I am on top of my game. *Well, not so much.*

One of the comical things about living off grid with a lot of woods around your house is that emails sent from your phone don't always get through. You might not know for a few days that they did not make it. It's just one of those things. So, my original sub plans did not go through. Fortunately, I text-messaged Diane, the principal's secretary and let her know that I was feeling really dizzy and was seeing stars and that Mike was taking me to the doctor at 8. That, she got.

Mike picked up the doctor's note the following morning and also picked up some workbooks I had on my desk that I could use to create sub plans for my students. The school nurse said, "Yep, she's out all week." That was it. Done. Diane put the information into my employee account. After that, there was no pushing through, no busying through, no going in. I was out.

Okay. You see it happen. People who just never say no and can't stop being useful. I don't see it as a sickness. I see it as a gift. I recently watched a TedTalk by Michael Jr., a comedian, and his punch line was that the minute he started to realize that he was no longer trying to "get laughs from people and started thinking of it as giving people an opportunity to laugh," he knew he had it. Michael Jr. spoke about delivering comedy routines to homeless shelters, centers for abused children, and jails. He schedules a show in one of those places in every city after every regularly scheduled paid show. He's good. He told a story of an abused boy from a shelter who never spoke and believed that if he wore his Spiderman costume over his face, it would protect him from his mother who pulled his toenails out as punishment.

Michael Jr. said, by about the middle of his routine, the boy moved up to him, removed his facemask and said, "Hi, my name is Roland." And continued talking for nine minutes as though there wasn't a show going on.

There is so much need out there for people to just love each other. None of the how's or the why's matter. If we're given an opportunity to make a difference in one person's life, what an honor to be able to just get out there and do it. It's as humble an act as being able to say, "Hey, there is somebody here who cares. This person, WILL take this home with her and will discuss you with her husband over dinner and they'll talk about small things that they might be able to do to help you." Maybe it's a new pair of eyeglasses. Maybe it's just that look in the eye the next day that says, "I care." I know it's not something that you can just pretend.

The funny thing is that when you are used to giving, you're not always that great at receiving. That's when being sick comes along and just takes you out. It takes those dark places in the mind, the ones that tell you how worthless you are, makes them center stage drama, and then invites all of your friends to the play. The awesome thing is that instead of booing you off stage for your crappy drama, they come and place flowers at your feet.

When you love someone, it doesn't matter that sometimes their drama is unconvincing and trite. What matters to you is that it is their drama, and they need your flowers, not your boos.

Being out gave me an opportunity to reflect on the incredible opportunity I have to work in a school. I have always said that teachers are the absolute best people I have ever had the chance to work with. They are overwhelmingly kind and giving. You have to be if you want to last more than a few years in the job. They say a broken heart works best. All teachers work with broken hearts.

Being out gave me a new perspective on my kids. I am truly honored to have this kind of job where I can offer a kind word, a truism, a hug, and yes, sometimes an office referral. Sometimes the greatest act of love is that office referral because it would have been so much easier to just give that person another try but you know that the next time it will be worse. There are lots of ways to say you care. And school is the place where we say it all day long.

Some of my students sent special messages when Mike went in to deliver my doctor's note. All of the messages were unsolicited and heartfelt. Working in a school is a place where a teacher goes through life's challenges in such a public way. When our children get sick, our parents pass on, or we deal with our own illnesses, they notice, because well, we're out.

In every case I can think of, the school community is where help begins to take place. There is the casserole committee, the support for families who have had fires, people battling cancer, fundraisers for all manner of needs. Quick conversations between gulping down lunch and waiting for the bathroom before the bell rings mean a lot.

Being out also helped me to appreciate my husband a little more. There he was downstairs, chopping up leeks because he knows I like them in my chicken soup. It was 8:35 p.m. and he had just come in from an hour drive from Greenville for softball practice after working all day refurbishing an old house that his friend is converting into apartments. He's on drywall, which, if you've ever done drywall, you know can be a beast because of all of the dust. But, he learned from Skip, an expert dry-waller, on a community service job we did for our town, how to drywall with barely any dust. So, he says it's not that bad as long as he can do the mudding. And there he is, after an incredibly long day with dust in his hair, in the kitchen, making me chicken soup the way I like it.

When it was done, he brought it up to me on a tray with a tall glass of water. We ate dinner together in bed and talked about his athletes, their needs, their potentials, where there may be some potential for trouble and how to get to it before it brews. They are looking at a good chance for the state title and every girl counts. I take a minute to send emojis or gifs to some of the kids who like hearing that coach said they did a great job tonight. It is a good way to end a day.

I guess every life conducts its chapters in strange order. Some chapters don't end up in the final book. I didn't want to end Book III with being out but stuff happens and the beautiful part about being human is how real it all is and we love each other anyway. There is never any point in trying to pretend that we are anything but who we are. That knowledge creates a solid ground under us so that no matter where we find ourselves, no matter the chapter we are in at the moment, we are real.

STINGING NETTLE

After a bout with illness, a person's immune system must be given a chance to regenerate. That means a lot of rest, healthy food, and good teas. In my book, tea is as important as food. It will not provide calories unless it is sweetened with honey or maple syrup but it will provide much of the phytonutrients the body needs for recovery.

One of the teas that Mike and I use for an immune booster is stinging nettle. Some people refer to the plant as Grandmother Nettle. I think of nettle as mettle. It provides the extra strength and protection against much of what can bug us. Since we can all agree that stress is bad for the immune system, we can, therefore, logically agree that when a person's emotions get upset or out of balance, dis-ease or ill-ness can ensue.

In its plant form, stinging nettle has little hairs that can penetrate a human's bare skin and causes a burning irritation. (We have a salve that provides immediate relief but that is for another day.) Unlike poison ivy, which is an oil that spreads, can cling to clothing, enter the lungs, and will linger for days, the hot rash of stinging nettle will pass in a matter of hours.

This very quality is the beauty of Grandmother Nettle. She knows how to keep her boundaries but is merciful in her delivery.

The other wonderful thing about stinging nettle is that once it is washed, cooked, or dried, the little stinging hairs no longer sting. Many people use nettle as a pot green (no, no one smokes it). You put it in soups and dishes much like you would spinach. It contains more minerals like iron, potassium, and manganese and more vitamins like C, K, and some of the B's than spinach. It also contains the rare vitamin B-12 that most plants do not.

Most people who use nettle to boost their strength and immune systems will either take it in a gel cap from the health food store or they will drink it as a tea. Some of us who live on the wild side do not mind allowing a piece of our yards to get a little overgrown by nettle, however the sting. Grandmother Nettle is bountiful and does like to spread her arms out, that's for sure. The best way to make her happy is to take her bounty and use it to keep our bodies strong. Being strong can help us keep our emotional boundaries up, as well. That could help with the dis-ease.

Epilogue
June 3, 2018

    I awoke to the knocking sound of a woodpecker. Mike and I had been hearing its distinctive call for a couple of weeks now. The world was silent except for the knock, knock, knocking of this powerful little bird.

    I thought how wonderful it is to have no sense of traffic or human noise other than Mike's breathing to awaken me. The woodpecker represents the rhythms of nature and our lives. It is the sacred drum, the heartbeat, the breath. To me it also represents the awakening of consciousness, the opening of a new day.

    These are the kinds of subtleties I need to function properly. I must hear the birds. If ever the world gets so noisy that I can no longer hear the birds, I must excuse myself for a time. The honest truth is that the pervasive world noise amplifies the noise inside my own head.

About that meditative kind of listening, Mike says, "I don't need to sit around to do it. I guess I am meditating while I work." He has taught me much about forgiveness, unconditional love, and being present in the moment. When Mike and I talk about how he learned to listen to his spirit without much external guidance, he tells me that it is because he spends so much time in quiet while he is working. It gives him time to think.

My job as a teacher is the antithesis of this work environment. If I am not careful, this noisy multitasking world can eat up the quiet world we both worked so hard to establish out here. It can consume Mike's hard-earned world too, if I let it.

He told me a story of a man who ran a factory for a living and every day before he entered his house, he would stick his hand in the bush next to his front door. He would repeat the process on his way out the next morning as he headed off to work. One day the man's son asked him why he did that.

"Son, every evening before I walk through the doors of our home, I hang my job up on a little hanger I keep in that bush. In the morning when I reach for it, it's right there where I left it so I never have to worry that I will forget it when I head out to work in the morning."

My friend Happy says that *work* is a four-letter word. For many of us, our jobs might inspire a few curse words on occasion, but most of us are grateful that we have work and that because of it, we can provide for our needs and the needs of our families.

Keeping it Real means being able to hang up the noisy disturbances before entering the door. It doesn't mean that I don't talk about it. It means that I leave the mental mechanics, the worry, and the insecurities by the door before I go home so that I can be fully present for my spouse.

Living in the quiet, as we do now, provides a backdrop of peace that makes all of the mental noise so glaringly obvious that carrying it home with you is like dumping garbage in a pristine environment. Perhaps what I need to work on is first, reducing the amount of garbage I bring home, and second, hanging it up in its place so that it doesn't spill everywhere.

Living off-grid gives us the luxury to hear the silence broken only by the rhythm of a woodpecker at work, providing for himself and his future family. I learned from my birder friend, Josh, that the woodpeckers open holes that the hummingbirds use later to extract worms and insects when their hatchlings need the concentrated protein to grow strong enough to leave the nest. We are all interconnected, and while our work provides for us and our families, it is opening up opportunities for others to provide for themselves too.

As Mike and I move into our next phase of life, our work has led us to a State Championship, organizing a student and teacher trip to Costa Rica, made us more comfortable, able to save for future adventures, and even more conscious of *Hearing the Silence*.

Michele Maingot Cabral spent her formative years climbing trees with pocket knives and notebooks in the United States and the West Indies. Her interest in writing journals, essays, and poetry continued into adulthood. For close to two decades, she held a career as a Nationally Board Certified high school English teacher and holds a Masters in English Education. She presently teaches Spanish in a local high school.

She lives with her husband, Mike, and their dog, Hermes, in an off-grid cabin they built together in the woods of Maine. Along with teaching, she writes, teaches yoga, swings a hammer, keeps bees, and forages for a living. She and Mike also created a line of salves and soaps that they sell locally.

She is the author of four books (*Walking Away, Making it Home,* and *Keeping it Real)* in the series, *Waking up from the American Dream.* She also authored an adult coloring book/journal entitled *A Simple Wayfarers's Book of Open Meditations.*

She is presently working on Book IV of the *Waking up from the American Dream* series entitled, *Hearing the Silence.*